BETWEEN ROARS AND RIGORS

Rajan Prasad Pokharel

PublishAmerica
Baltimore

First printing

PublishAmerica has allowed this work to remain exactly as the author intended, verbatim, without editorial input.

Softcover 9781462611218
PUBLISHED BY PUBLISHAMERICA, LLLP
www.publishamerica.com
Baltimore

Printed in the United States of America

Foreword

In 2011 alone, my two books ***Rebels of the Mountains*** and ***Beyond the Life Lines*** got published from the USA. In the process of becoming a writer, my responsibility certainly grew about getting myself known to my readers. Through the present book ***Between Roars and Rigors***, I am trying to throw some light upon my own life.

Being a new writer of the art of fiction, I have learned that a creation of a character of the work of art is a very complicated task. A single character of a fiction is the reflections of many more characters of a real life world. In order to draw a complete fictional character, I have to bring the images of many real characters in my imaginations and put their striking features and events in a single frame-work. At some gaps and lapses, I am bound to give the glimpses from my own life also. Even then I cease to become a good writer when my characters do not grow.

Therefore, all the people I have met, and interacted or befriended with have been very useful for the projection of the character's personalities in my works. The real people in my reminiscences have the significant roles in the sketch of the characters. My memoirs and my experiences are the most important raw materials for my creative imaginations. In this sense, the broader the horizon of life I develop, the sharper the presentations I can, therefore, make. For a writer no experience, whether pleasant or painful, is useless. But the most important thing is how far the creative writer can magnify or transform his/ her experiences.

In this book I have made all my autobiographical traces in the forms of stories and essays. In this course I have deeply realized that a writer's personality is shaped by a wide range of reminiscences and vast experiences which are directly or indirectly reflected in his or her writings. A writer's autobiography is, therefore, probably the most important thing to understand his or her works. I have sincerely ransacked the events and images through my most personal reminiscences and have presented them here afore.

At this moment I must thank my High School head master Mr. Subarna Bahadur Thapa who put the foundation of my language learning upon which I developed an edifice by the continuous support of my teacher, my supervisor and my great inspirer Prof. Dr Shreedhar Prasad Lohani who always encouraged me for a good writing. I am most thankful to him.

I should like to thank Dr Shreedhar Gautam and Mr Bharat Pokharel for their regular encouragement. I must thank my friends Madan Adhikari and Uddhav Rai who have always supported me towards this direction. I am sincerely thankful to my seniors, my colleagues, my cousins, my friends, my siblings and my children for their great supports.

I must be most grateful to my mother who showed me this world, reared me and geared to this level. I must thank my wife to have always energized me to this course. Thanks.

Rajan Prasad Pokharel (Ph.D.)
Associate Professor
Patan Multiple Campus, TU, Nepal
Current Address: Brampton, Canada
Email address: rajanppokharel@gmail.com

Chapter One
Fears and Fancies

It was the month of July, the month of paddy plantation. Everybody had gone to the paddy land. Kumar bro took me to the field where plantation was going on. On the way there was another exciting plantation ceremony taking place. We had to pass across the area. I was probably three years old then to be singing some catchy songs in my sweet children's jargon. Most of the people there working in the field were from the local Kirats (Rais). They were singing and working.

Kumar bro attracted the attention of the people there telling them that I too could sing a sweet song. Then, everybody told me to sing a song. In excitement I sang the song that I had memorized which meant like: 'Jite's son Manaraje runs away with Dhanasiri.' It was a kind of scandal in the village that Manaraje would elope with Dhanasiri, somebody's wife. Surprisingly enough in the same field on that day Manaraje and Dhanasiri's husband too were present there. On listening to the song Manaraje ran to me shouting with a khukuri in his hand threatening me that he would chop my body apart. I ran away screaming and crying. Others stopped Manaraje from coming close to me. I now realize that it was such an embarrassing situation to them and dreadful to me which still makes me feel most fugitive even to remember such a difficult time. I had learned the song from Kumar bro himself.

Kumar bro was an indispensable part of my life in those days. His mother had eloped with someone leaving him and his younger brother behind. Therefore, they used to live with the maternal grandparents and uncles. Being my father's sister's children and my cousin brothers, I was in their company every time sharing my earliest childhood notions and jargons.

I remember that I had a small cat which I loved very much. Unfortunately on one morning I found it cold and motionless. I told Kumar bro, and he told the grand mother. She concluded that it was dead. I violently cried in my extreme shock. Then finally Kumar bro carried it in a bamboo basket and I followed him down to the edge of our land. I went crying behind Kumar bro throughout its funeral procession. We dug the ground and buried it.

The cat was really loving and friendly to me. It too was small like a child, and it used to understand my language. It used to play with me excitingly as if we too shared our most intimate feelings. I would care it very much, and both of us used to eat together. If it went out to the field or to the kitchen garden, I too would follow it and Kumar bro too used to follow both of us, and if there was any problem in getting it back from a steep and bushy ridge, my grandmother would come behind us. Finally my grandfather would come and get us all back.

The cat seemed to understand my interests, intentions and activities, and would try to slip out to hide itself from me. When I would start crying, it would say "Meuo!" I would follow its sound and finally catch it. If I did not find it at one search, it would give a repeated signal, "Meuo! Meuo!" I would be in a tension and return to it with its sound as if I had understood him, "Meuo! Meuo! Meuo! Where are you? Come on. Come out. I want to see you right now. Don't trouble me, my dear! I cannot tolerate your absence so long." Then it would creak out through the dry leaves and broken twigs. I would lift it with love, kiss it, slowly rub on its body and bring it back at the courtyard and say, "What a nice, sweet, lovely and small kitten you are! I love you. I cannot live without you." In response to my feeling, it would say, "I too cannot. I too cannot. Meuo! Meuo! Meuo!"

I lost such a lovely kitten. I was badly shocked and frustrated. In some days my attention was diverted to some other things. But its memory remained firmly stamped in my mind. I was growing. I started going to the barn with Kumar bro and sometimes also to graze cattle to the nearby fields.

One night a tiger grabbed away a baby calf from our barn. My grandfather was shocked. The cow turned totally hostile to give the milk. Then my grandfather asked a cobbler to make an artificial calf from the old leather, and he did. Then the cow licked on the body on the simulating calf, and we milked the cow, but sometimes it was suspicious probably to see that the artificial calf did not move and jump around the mother as the real calf used to do. The cow looked upset for hours.

One day the cattle were passing along a narrow trail on the hill side. The calf-less cow had been looking lost for some days. It was behaving very strangely and unnaturally. It probably was in its subconscious mind or in a trauma. Suddenly it slipped through a steep hill and slid down to the foothills on the river bank to its death. Today, I feel confused to think whether it met its casual death, or it deliberately committed suicide on the loss of its sweet baby calf! But for me, the loss of the calf, the death of the cow and the sudden demise of my sweet little kitten still remain deeply traumatic in my mind.

It was another startling reminiscence of those very early days that bites me badly sometimes. I was three years old and my brother was just born at that time. My father had gone to the farm house across the river. While coming back when he was about to cross the river, suddenly right at that time a landslide fell and he was hit by a big boulder on his legs. He fell down and a part of land-slides covered him below the waist. When he recovered his consciousness, he found himself totally trapped, motionless and vulnerable. Then he whistled with his tongue. He whistled several times. Some villagers recognized my father's way of whistling. They came to my grandfather. In curiosity they went to the hill side to see what had happened. Then they put the stones and mud aside from him, and brought him home in a locally made stretcher. They put a bamboo plaster with some medicinal herbs around his broken leg and some domestic creams on the injured parts. For about four months he lay down in bed and got a kind of recovery. One of his legs turned shorter than the other. He was healed well, but there was an apparent mark like a big boil on his broken leg.

In those days I did not know anything about the mishap and its possible consequences, but now I bite my tongue to think what would have happened to us if my father had not recovered his consciousness from the deadly hit!

I was probably seven years old and my second brother was just four. My sister was in the lap of the mother. My father had been to the plain land of the South (Madhes) about seven hills away. We suffered a big famine. There was not a single grain of corn in our house. My mother sent me and my little brother to another hill village to buy some millet. I had to carry about ten kilos and my brother about six kilos. It was really a very tough time for us to bring the millet home. My brother suffered from diarrhea for some days, and the mother was really tense.

After some days, my mother left the sister in my care and went with the small brother to another hill village in order to collect the money back from a Kirat which my father had given to him on a loan. While coming back, the water level of the river had already risen. The mother tied the brother on her body with her shawl and dared to cross the river. But they were swept away by the river and they both lost their consciousness. After a while my brother felt a stone beside and pulled it with his both hands drawing the mother to the side. Then the mother recovered her consciousness and slowly got up. Both of them kept waiting on the riverside for the water level to go down praying to all thirty three millions of gods and goddesses. The water level lowered about an hour later, and they crossed the river. At home my sister was so hungry that I did not have anything to feed her. I went to the nearby field, reaped some raw paddy, fried it, and rubbed it on the stone with another stone and cooked some oatmeal and fed her.

My mother and brother came home trembling with fear. The mother told me the story and said that they survived luckily. She also said that my small brother saved her too. The mother took over the care of the sister. Then after a while my brother and I went to play outside. What would I have done if the mother had not come home back? I feel dreaded even to remember the situation.

Many times in my life I have come across the state of hallucinations. When I slept in the day time and got up after the sun set before the dusk, my mother used to tell me that I slept quite long from midday to the next morning. Then I would just wash my face, brush my teeth and would be ready to move away either to school or to graze the cattle or to fetch the grass. And then my mother would stop me saying that she was just joking. Likewise, many times I have had the hallucinations of ghosts, spirits and ghostly scarecrows moving around me or in the distance upon the dark images of a tree, a bush, a wooden pillar or some animals. I fell sick at the sight of them and also realized that I had the hallucinations. Similarly, I had had the hallucinations about witches and witch-crafts too.

The hallucinations of such supernatural concepts have been inherently inculcated in our minds for the last several generations. Different from those types, I got a strange hallucination once. I was in my class in a primary school in the hill side. I could be just seven or eight years old. I knew the teacher was teaching in the class. Suddenly I spoke out calling my mother, "Mother! Have you fixed the cow in its place in the barn?"

The teacher was really surprised, and he stood staring at me for a while. He then stopped the class and took me in the office. He and other teachers asked me very simple questions, but I could not answer any. They gave me a book to read, but I could not read even a single word. Then the teacher sent me home along with some friends. I was going down, but I thought I was going up. I thought that I was going up to my mother's sister's house with my little brother. I told him, "My little brother! Follow me carefully. You may fall down." Actually I was going down home with my friends. At home the friends reported everything to my mother. The mother took me to sleep. After some hours I came to the normal situation. I resumed all my memory and consciousness.

For two days I didn't go to school. Later the villagers concluded that I had got the intoxication of the honey of the spring season which my mother had got from the bees' hive just in the morning of that day. I had eaten my food with a good amount of honey. It was nothing other than a sheer intoxication of the spring day honey. But I got a strange and unique experience of hallucination in my childhood, which is worth mentioning here. At ten of my age we migrated to the plain lands of the south from the hill side. Then, from there began the real days of my adventures, excitements and sufferings.

Chapter Two
Migration

I told my father, "Baa! Purush says that he too wants to go to Madhes with us. He says that he talked to his grandparents that he wants to go to live with his parents in Madhes. But he says that he does not have his shoes."

My father said, "Ok, no problem! He should not worry. I will buy a pair of shoes for him at Arkhoule bazaar. Tell him that he can join us, or if his grandparents too talked to me, it would be much better."

We prepared for our migration. My father sold the cattle and told the neighbouring uncles to till the land and also look after the empty house till another settlement. My younger brother and I went to the school and told the teachers and friends that we were migrating. We went to the friends' and relatives' houses that we were going to Madhes.

My mother had the most sensible relationship with other women of the village. Mother was rather shocked and serious about our moving. Early in the morning on the day, our porters came to carry the specially prepared baskets on their backs. They had their supportive sticks in their hands and matted ropes on their heads and shoulders to carry the burdens. My father put water on the mud buckets both sides on the doorsteps that symbolically meant for a good journey. As we just stepped out, my father chanted some Sanskrit verses for a good move. My mother could not stop herself. She burst out in tears and started crying loudly. Together other women who had come to see us off too cried. As we passed by every house, my mother and other women of the village shared tears and cries with the feeling of the uncertainty of the journey of life. They promised that they would meet some day if they remained alive.

I had my old bag on my back and stick in my hand. I was rather excited by this journey. Purush and his grandparents were waiting for us on the way. My father and his grandparents talked for a while, and Purush too moved with us. My mother was crying all the way through the village till we got into the jungle and houseless meadows of the up-hills.

It was the morning time. The winter had just begun. The ground on the way was very cold. I felt that my friend Purush was not being able to walk. I told my father about his problem. Then till Arkhoule bazaar, Purush and I put on the same pair of shoes turn by turn. He put them on for about a kilometre and I wore them for almost like another kilometre. Whenever we found any fire on the log beside the trail, we warmed our hands and legs for a while and then again ran to catch the family and the porters.

On our way to Madhes we met hundreds of people coming and going up the narrow trails. My father told us stories to make our movement easier. We had had seven nights on the way sheltering some times on the hill tops, sometimes on the riverbanks and sometimes even in the middle of the jungle but with many other travellers around.

One night we could not move with other travellers and it so happened by chance that our family and the porters had to settle on a hill side above the river. Down below the steep hill was a deep blue river. It was such a lonely place that there were no houses around probably in the distance of about ten kilometres. It was a jungle area also. The porters told us the stories that they had heard that the robbers would cross the river by their boats and loot the travellers in those areas. After the meal the porters had a camp fire and they slept in their turns one after another.

My father too remained awake till midnight. I pretended to sleep, but those dreadful stories kept me almost all night awake. I thought that I would sleep the next night with a full rest. The other day we could not cover up a long distance. My father said that it was better to have a better shelter than walking a long way up. When we had to walk up and down the hill, we would be sad, but when we were to walk on a straight way or in the plain areas, we would be happy. On the river banks, we would run with excitement.

On a residential area on the top of a hill, my brother suddenly saw a hen moving complacently with its newly hatched chickens. He had a stick in his hand. He suddenly ran to the hen and struck on it with the stick. The hen fluttered away with its chicken in a dreaded sound towards a house. My father snatched the stick from his hand. As we had walked a little bit farther, some villagers came and stopped us. They took my father to a house, and in front of a man compelled him to pay the price of the hen and its chickens. My father did not speak anything, but paid for their claim and cleared out the way ahead. He did not even slightly scold my younger brother who could be simply about seven then.

The journey continued frequently resting on the well-raised pedestals under the trees. My mother told us to keep pace with the porters. The porters were very fast. They were in hurry also, because they had to carry the loads of many more migrating teams in the season and had to earn as much as to sustain for the whole year. And because of the slow moving family with the small children, they had to wait for us at a certain distance with sufficient rest to kill their tiredness.

My friend Purush and I were tense. Sometimes on the easy, straight and plain way of the river bank, we tried to walk along with the porters, but we had to run, and we got tired soon. And then we dropped and moved with the parents in the pace of the small children.

It was really delightful to walk along a plain trail even for a mile. I imagined how good it would be to walk in the plain roads for miles; and Madhes is plain, easy and beautiful. I thought I would enjoy Madhes very much. I would go to school in Madhes and join in grade five and study as high as to grade ten like the teachers in the hill side schools. I too would be a teacher after a normal training. Normal training was a very famous term in the schools for a teacher to be. I actually did not know its meaning but the term used to sound beautiful to me.

For miles on our journey, down the foot trail there was a deep blue river. It was a branch of the Sapta Koshi (a river of seven big rivers). Seven rivers from different sides in the eastern hills get mixed in Sapta Koshi River, which is supposed to be probably the biggest river of Nepal. We followed Doodh Koshi and saw the confluences of Arun, Tamor, Indrawati, Tama Koshi, Sun Koshi and Bhote Koshi and many other small rivers on our way. The river looked bluer, wider, fuller and slower as it went bigger and bigger. I asked my mother why it was so. She said, "The bigger the man is, the gentler and more polite he is. That is the symbol of greatness." Purush and I were convinced well with much enlightenment. Every time we saw a river getting into another river, I would ask my mother, "Mother! How deep would it be like now?"

My mother said, "It would be like a full bamboo deep now, or a one and half bamboo deep." Then my friend, brother and I would open the mouth and show the whole tongue out to exclaim, "One and half bamboo deep! Oh, my goodness! How so deep it is!"

And then, overwhelmed by the thought of a deep intimacy with those rivers, I told my friend Purush, "See, this river contains the water of Kalleri River, Ambote River and Rawa

River too. Forget that we have been walking along a big branch of Sapta Koshi River. We are with the same rivers of our closeness. Can't you think in that way?" They were the nearest rivers from our hill village, on the banks of which I passed most part of my childhood walking, swimming, playing on their banks, grazing cattle, and fetching water in the bamboo vessels to the barn house.

Purush too would jump with excitement and if there were shallow banks somewhere in the general people's reach on the way, we would both run to the river and wash our face and sprinkle water on our head with deep respect and love. My father would warn that we would slip into the depth, and get drowned. We would defend that we would go to those places only where other people too would go for their wash. We said that we were extremely careful.

We finally crossed the Sapta Koshi River by a big boat slightly above Chatara near Barahchhetra. There were stories of capsized boats, and the boats men told us to sit firmly in proper balance within the boat not stretching our bodies outside. Even then I managed to touch the water and put it on my head thinking that River Kalleri would save us. I murmured, "Dear Mother Kalleri! Save us!"

I saw my father and the porters too touching the water once or twice in the emotional attachment and excitement. I imagined that the boat being capsized, and we all dead. I thought, "In that situation my father alone would probably swim across. He would be deeply shocked, and he would weep, cry, mourn and finally accept the tragedy. For many days he would be confused. He would call me, my brothers and my sister with love. He would suddenly wake up in his dream to try to carry my little sister on his shoulder with love but in vain. He would wipe his face and drink water. He would travel to many places telling people the story of his tragedy. And then in Madhes he would marry again, and have a new family and children. We would be just in his memory as a trauma." I imagined in that way, because I had heard several stories of the likes.

Slightly above the Chatara town from a ridge, we watched the jeep vehicles running. The movement really charmed me. In my early childhood too, I had been to Madhes and had been even to India with my father. I remember that I had been lost in the train when my father had been to fetch water and he could not catch the same bogie. I cried for about an hour till my father recovered me. I feel startled and scared even to remember the dreadful moments. I have had lot many imaginations about the idea to think what would have happened if my father had not found me back. The series of imaginations would probably amount to volumes. I don't go to that complicated sphere now.

Anyway, Chatara town looked majestic in the hours of sunset. We were so much excited. I don't remember how I shouted and what song I might have sung at the vision of Madhes in the conscious but still an innocent stage of my childhood. I am still an expert of randomly singing the sung - unsung songs in my own musical whims and wandering thoughts. Purush was one or two years older than me, and he had been to Madhes about a couple of times before. He said that he would catch a jeep to Chakkarghatti, and he would reach home easily.

Purush departed from me. A friend with whom I had some most interesting moments left me. I was sad, but we had to move fast because another vehicle too was ready to carry us to Dharan. My father said that we would have a night halt in Dharan itself. The porters too received their payment and left us.

Chatara town looked really gorgeous and beautiful. The crowd of the market, the hasty vehicles and business-like manners and noises of the people charmed me. By a public vehicle in the evening we got down in Dharan city which was much bigger, busier and more business-like than Chatara. My father unfolded our beds under an open terrace of a house near a school gate. Somebody came and showed us a public shelter behind the school. That night we had beaten rice and milk porridge that we had carried in our bags. My father brought some ready-made food for us, especially for my little sister. Next day we took a bus, got down at a station, hired a bullock cart and then finally reached a village in Madhes where we were supposed to settle down.

My uncles' families were already there. I was not familiar with my cousins too. I had only heard about them. They all gathered around us. I distributed some sweet balls to them. After a while, a cousin who was of the same age of mine called me. I followed him. He took me along a paddy field. Down at the end was a barren land near the bush. He took me there and said, "See, I dug here and made a small paddy field, and myself planted some rice and harvested it just last month. I sold the paddy and made three rupees. I will help you make another paddy field there and you too will make money, Ok?"

I guessed the structure of my life in the days to come. I said, "Ok!" Then we ran towards home. My other cousins too followed us. They told me about the paddy fields, bushes, playgrounds and villages around. I was happy to think that I would be using a vast space of Madhes around.

Chapter Three
The Space

Next day my father taking me by the arm told some of my cousins, "Boys! Help this boy. He can make a good friend of you. Take him to your school. He wants to study. Hey, girls! Love my children. They want to grow with you." The cousins nodded their heads. I came to know that many of my cousins were not going to school. After the morning meal my cousins took me to the paddy fields to search out the left-over of the paddy grains. I too did the same with them. We went away from home. The paddy fields sprawled far and wide in large plots. We had had our linen bags safely hung on the cross shoulders. I too collected almost a kilogram of the rice out of the hay-straws, bundles and stacks. Later back at home, a cousin gave me a bucket in which I put the day's collections.

Then we went to collect some banana flowers and black ferns. We hooked the banana flowers from the banana bushes and brought them home for curry and pickles. In some days my father erected a small hovel and a barn, and managed to have a pair of oxen and a cow. I too shunned the cattle with my cousins into the open fields. The left-over collection of rice was no more after few weeks. The same year many other people migrated to our village and to the surrounding villages. We got naturally mixed up with their children. Then we too drove our cattle to graze with other children's cattle together.

There were large grass lands, meadows, barren fields, river banks, bushes and hedges. Many pieces of lands were left uncultivated due to the shortage of irrigation and lack of working man power. The new people had bought some pieces of land, and many others occupied the uncultivated areas. Then the number of habitations and residential areas grew significantly.

There were villages of tribesmen. They hesitated mixing up with the new comers due to their language, culture and fear. We met them quite often in the fields and local markets. They would kill mice, squirrels, tortoises, birds and pheasants for their additional foods. They would also collect small water snails for eating. Early in the morning the tribal women would come out with their fishing nets and collect fish for their meals. During their festivals, a large number of people from the tribal groups would go to the rivers, ponds and swampy wet lands for the collection of fish.

It would always be a wonderful sight to watch how they fished together singing and dancing. The way they would go to the local bazaars and fairs, the way they had the weddings and the way they celebrated festivals were really strange and wonderful. Most of the paddy fields were being cultivated by those local tribesmen, no matter who were the owners. They themselves possessed small pieces of lands or no lands, but they thought that they were the real masters of the spaces all around.

In course of time we too could understand their languages and cultures, and also managed to communicate somehow in their languages too. They too started speaking in our language with the mixture of their own words.

In a couple of months of our migration to the village, I met a boy who too wanted to go to school. But the schools were not near. The nearest middle school too was at least three kilometres away from our village. The boy's family had not come there directly from the hills. They had been at different villages in the plain lands before and were moving to several other villages in search of better living and better communities.

The boy and I decided to go to school. The first school that I attended in Madhes was Karenuwa School in the middle of the Tharus' villages. Tharus are the tribal people of Nepalese plain lands of the south. Almost all teachers and students were Tharus. They would mostly speak in their own language. Later on, the teachers started speaking in the Nepali language also and slowly and gradually the students too practised speaking. Anyway, we understood each other's languages by gestures and in words reciprocally.

My friend was a very clever boy. He would always carry his linen gown cover. Under it he would conceal some rice and mustard and sell it in the local merchant's shop without his parents' knowledge. On the first day in school when the classes were going on, he asked me to scrawl some letters on his back, and he would recognize them howsoever cursive I wrote. I wrote some alphabet and he tried to guess also, but after a while I looked at his face thinking why he was not speaking. Surprisingly enough he felt comfortably sleepy from the way I scratched on his back and he was already asleep. I came to know that it was his trick to fall asleep in class. I guessed that he must have befooled many other class mates in his previous schools in that way. His name was RN.

My friend RN never did his home works, or the class works. If he got a chance of going out for pee in the midst of the class, he would not come back to the class for half an hour. He was probably two or three years older than me. Even at his twelve or thirteen he had learned to smoke and use the chewing tobacco. The teacher knew that he was a discrepant, restless and cunning student. Everybody knew his shrewdness. Sometimes the class teachers punished him physically with a local fiddle which could be used for driving the oxen to pull the carts. Its leather strings were long with the knots on the end. RN was usually with his gown cover, and when the teacher whipped him, the knots of the fiddle would strike on my back and I used to tolerate silently. When the teacher used more power, he would order me to move away. Sometimes the teacher would drag RN to the front of the class in a wider space and beat him violently. Even then RN never cried or reacted. He would not speak anything except that he pretended why he had no time in doing the works.

One day RN told me that there was the king's visit in Biratnagar, and we should slip out from the school. He said that he had stolen some wheat from his home, and with that money both of us would manage to make a two way trip. I was convinced, and without telling anybody about our running away, we went to Biratnagar.

The buses were very much crowded and the whole city of Biratnagar was full of welcome rallies and support demonstrations for the king organized by the-then Panchayat machincries. We were lost in the crowd. We ran here and there, but did not have even a single glance upon the king. In the evening there was no place for us to eat and stay. We tried to catch the buses back home, but they were really very much crowded. The spared money with him too had been over, because we had some snacks during the day. Finally at about eight in the evening we managed to get into a crowded bus, but after two stations away, the fare collector pushed us down. When the bus was about to pull away, RN cried loudly saying "Baa! My father is there in the bus."

The bus stopped again. My friend said that his father was there in the bus. The bus staff inquired the passengers loudly to tell him if any body's child was missing. When nobody spoke, the bus left us there and ran away.

There was no light on the road side. It was about ten at night. We walked along the road and after about a mile's walk we moved to a residential area. We were afraid that we would be knocked down by the dogs or people would misunderstand us as thieves and charge us. We moved to a court of the paddy field where paddy bundles were collected in piles and stacks. Some boys were sleeping in a hay-hut in order to guard the collection. We went close and asked them, "Brothers! Can we too sleep beside you? We got lost and got down at a wrong station. We are suffering from chilling cold."

They told us that we could sleep beside and share the rugs also. But almost for the whole night we were sexually tortured by each of them turn by turn. Early in the next morning before the boys had got up, we ran away. I was shivering with cold, hunger and weakness. I felt that I would collapse. We found an oxen cart creaking on the way, and asked the cart man to give us a lift. It was empty also. He showed his kindness to us. He gave a sugar cane for us to bite and chew. I felt slightly relieved and drowsily took a nap on the cart itself. After an hour RN got me up. We had to walk on foot up the way home. I felt difficult in walking, because of the effects of the overnight torture by the boys in the hay-hut. When I reached home, my mother asked me where I had gone. I told her that the school management committee had taken us for the rally in the king's visit.

I fell sick for some days. RN dropped out the school and ran away from home. After RN had gone, I told my father to tell the uncles and send the cousins to school. Then I too changed the school. We all went to the same school together. Although some of my elder cousins started school much behind me, I found them exceptionally brilliant. All of them secured good positions in their classes till their matriculation. The school was some kilometres farther than the previous school. It was a high school from which I matriculated.

After twenty years I met RN in a bus terminal. I was waiting for a bus. Somebody came in front of me and said, "Do you remember me?" I recognized his sound but had forgotten his face. I ransacked various people in the files of my mind through different periods of the past. Suddenly he flashed in my mind and said, "'Oh! You are RN…! How are you? Where had you been for such a long period of time, man?"

He explained that he had been working as a staff in a public bus service. On the strength of the earning from the same job, he had bought a small house in the outskirt of the city where he and his family were living happily. He told me that his first son was studying in grade five and the second was in three. I congratulated him. I found a significant growth in his character. I had not thought that he would come up to that level also.

I told him that his son too was of the same stage of ours of those days. "Please, be careful. This is the most critical time for the children to shape up. Do you remember our days?" He got startled, and moved one step back in his sub-consciousness. He stretched his tongue out and became serious. He said, "My sons have gone the mother's way. She is a very good woman. I too have learned to go my wife's way."

I congratulated him once again. He got me a free ticket for my travel. On my journey I remembered the horrible days in his company. To remember those moments, my back ached and my anus burned deeply once again. I thanked time to have brought RN on the right course of life.

Chapter Four
The Roars

I went to school with my cousins. Like many other children we all went to school screaming, hooting, howling, playing, dancing, singing and sometimes even fighting. Even then there was a good coordination, and cooperation among us. Sometimes many other children of nearby villages too went with us together. It would be something like a rally on our way as far as to school.

In the hot season the school used to open in the morning time. We had to walk almost like five kilometres on foot. We did not have a watch or anything to confirm the time. We would wake up several times at midnight and look up in the sky to guess the time by the positions of certain groups of stars or during the lunar fortnights by the movement of the moon. Sometimes we would wake up just after midnights and move out for the morning classes. We generally would go through the nearby villages shouting to the friends to walk up together.

Those days in the villages very few people used to have clocks or watches. On the way if some body's parents guessed the time in the better way, we would rest there even for a couple of hours. Mostly we used to have such rests at Mohan- Prem's house whose elder brother Madan Bhandari later rose to the height a national leader and the General Secretary of CPN (UML) in the Nepalese politics. We had heard about him, but never had a chance to meet him. He had been underground for the formation and development of his party organization. Mohan and Prem were thorough gentlemen. They used to organize poetry symposiums, cultural programs and football tournaments in the village. I still have the fresh memories of those days in my mind as if we had had those moments just yesterday.

When the classes ran in the day time generally in the winter season, it was delightful to walk in the sunshine. We would cut short our way to the canal. The side-walks of the canal were like wide roads, and our senior cousin Manoj brother used to read out stories and novels to us, and we would enjoy reading them out turn by turn and listening to them. Those novels and short stories opened our horizon of knowledge and imagination wide. On the weekends and holidays and in the hot season basically after the school, we used to get our cattle out for grazing in the open fields. In the same way we used to read books of stories and English grammar for the collective benefit. The base of my English grammar is from the collective reading on the meadows and playgrounds.

We used the large space of the open lands and we made the best use of it for our funs and amusements. Back home from school we frequently changed the routes and went into the groves and bushes. We would have had our gats hidden under the mud or in the holes. Every time when we went back home from school, we would either have taken some nestlings of the doves or some fish or some jungle fruits or vegetables home. Those days a kind of banana was available everywhere which was planted by the land lords in order to feed their elephants. The bananas and their flowers were left all around. We would pull down the trunks and take the fruit and flower home without any body's permission.

It would be really delightful to steal mangoes from others' gardens. There used to be large groves and gardens of mangoes and other fruits in Madhes. "Hold on, hold on, don't go ahead. I will go and see if he is sleeping. He is lying there. Even if he is not asleep, I will talk to him. Two of you climb on the trees, and throw the mangoes in the field across the bush on the other side of the ridge of the brook-let. Ok?" A senior member would guide us.

"Yes, he is snoring. Go ahead as I told you. I will pretend to be searching in the ground if some mangoes have fallen. I will guard him. You will finish the work." He would say again. We would very carefully perform the mango stealing. He would again in a very low and stifled voice say, "Run away with the mangoes. He got up. I will talk to him about buying some pieces. You too get down and sneak away from the other side of the trunk of the tree. Be careful. Don't make haste. You will fall down."

"Hello bro! How are you? I was just scavenging here and there in the bushes if there were any half rotten fallen mangoes lying around. By the way do you sell some mangoes to me?" He would not have had any money; however he would just while away time with the owner or the watchman. Then he would beg one or two pieces of mangoes and slowly at first, and then a bit faster and finally still faster run to the friends where they would be hiding.

"Wait, wait. The yogi is not around. I will drink the palm juice directly from the pot and keep it hanging on the tree as it is." One of us would say. Another would naturally react, "No, I too want to drink. Untie the pot from the tree and run away. We will drink the whole lot turn by turn down there on the river side."

"See, there are several pots hanging on other trees too. Check them all and drink some portions from all of them." Then we would drink the crude palm juice directly collected from the trees and run away. But it would give us some kicks of tipsiness, and we would play on the way to pass time and then would go home. There was not a single garden or grove or a tree in about ten kilometres around our village from which we had not had any fruit. Many times we were badly dreaded or shooed away, and many times we escaped from being badly beaten.

We were coming back home from school during a morning class day. Manoj bro said, "Let's go to that grove and see if there are some mangoes fallen by the gusts of night time storm."

We said, "Ok, let's go." We went and saw a large number of bunches thickly hanging in clusters about to be ripe soon. We checked whether anybody was guarding or not. Surprisingly enough there was no body. Then, in order to grab the heavenly chances, the senior brothers Punya, Manoj, Lekhraj and Balkrishna climbed on to the trees and dropped the mangoes down. We forgot that that was not our garden. When there was a big amount, we realized that we had no bags. Then Punya and Manoj brothers sent us home to bring some bags and shacks without the parents' knowledge. The senior cousins looked after the heaps of mangoes. In a couple of hours when we came back with large bags, the brothers were dangerously running away. The owners of the grove chased them, and they luckily escaped. Otherwise, that day we all would have been whipped and slapped to a maximum extent.

Most of the times most of our cousins would be together playing, grazing cattle, cutting grass, going to school, swimming in the rivers, stealing fruits, going to local bazaars and having funs and joys. The company was really creative; but sometimes destructive too. One day in the afternoon we were playing near our homes. A neighbouring woman came and asked, "Good boys, help me. My daughter and son- in-law had come to me yesterday. But, I don't know what happened between them. They probably had some confrontation. In anger the son-in-law left the daughter and went away. Please, follow him and convince him, and bring him here! My daughter too is crying. I am in a problem. Please, help me, my dear good boys!"

We then immediately paid our serious attention to her request. She pointed out that in about a kilometre away, her son-in-law was moving fast. We all ran to bring him back. We shouted to him, "Stop. Please, stop. Don't run." But he still ran faster. The faster we ran, the more terrified he became and more speedily he ran again.

Then Punya bro told us, "Don't run. Some of you go down that way and cut short to the canal right before the bridge. Some go up the right, and try to catch him. We will pretend to walk slowly shouting, signalling and beckoning to him." Then the team disseminated to perform the genuine task. The man too had been tired. He looked back and saw that some of us were walking slowing without chasing him.

He stopped for a while probably thinking that we would not be able to catch him. Right at that time our boys had already gheraoed him. Our boys caught him firmly by the collars. The man forced to escape. Then the boys knocked him down. We all reached there from different positions. Then we picked him up, kicked him, slapped him on the cheeks and punched him on his nose as if he was a running criminal. His nose started bleeding. Then we brought him in front of his wife and the mother-in-law and threw down in the courtyard as if we were victorious in a fight with a villain.

To see his nose bleeding and his cheeks bruised and swelled up, and his cloth torn and body badly scratched, his wife suddenly sprang to him with love, clasped him and started crying in her deep attachment to him. His mother-in-law opened her mouth wide with her tongue flatly out in her complete surprise and picked a big bamboo rod to charge us in her extreme anger. In this way, we got the husband and wife united in their old emotional love, but my father paid for his treatment the other day.

After some days, the husband and wife went back to their home, but the old woman remained angry with us for a long time. Sometimes when she saw us, she would burst out in her harsh words upon us. But she never realized that we solved the problem between her daughter and son-in-law, otherwise anything might have happened in their relationship. Who knows? Later I realized that a bigger tension can naturally sweep away the smaller conflicts, but it is risky and definitely more painful.

Chapter Five
The Deadly Days

For many years we lived in a bamboo hut with a thatched roof. In the hill side we had a stony house much bigger than we needed, but in Madhes it was much smaller than we had to have. Expecting blissful days, we went on having worse ones every year. My mother gave birth to more brothers and sisters. We suffered from famine from the middle of the year. The days were really troublesome. Sometimes my mother and I slept hungry. The whole thing we could have in those days would be eaten up by the brothers and sisters. Father generally did not use to be home. He would come home after one or two months, and sometimes even in longer gaps. He was a bit of a carefree type of man and would randomly freak out with his friends and strangers for drinks and cards. Sometimes he would go to Kathmandu with so-called politicians.

That time father too was home. It was probably the month of April. A big storm blew at night and shook our house dangerously. Father hung on the roof to save it from being blown away, but he remained helpless and dropped the idea of hanging on the roof any more. The storm swept away the house. We all clustered to sit together beside a cot. My old grandmother was sleeping in the next room. The side bars had fallen on her bed, but luckily they got crossed in a shed, and my grand-mother was saved. Thereafter, it started raining heavily. Then my father jumped out shouting to his brothers to their houses, "Where are you? Come out to help me. My house got blown away. The bars fell on the mother's bed. I could not remove it. She is in a terrible condition. My children are dying. Come out soon."

Then all his three brothers came out and removed the side bars from the grandmother's place and took her to their house.

We all followed them and got safe that day. My fifth brother was on the mother's lap. We were slightly bigger than the smaller ones. My father had quarrelled with his brothers on a small piece of land about a couple of months ago, and had stopped speaking to them. The storm evoked a feeling of love between my father and his brothers.

I lost my books and notebooks. I recovered some of the books in a damaged condition from the field about two hundred meters away. I never found a grammar book which I had been reading and practicing seriously. My grammar would have been a bit better if I had finished practicing that old high school Nesfield version.

My father collected the roof back and erected a bamboo hut again, but the season had been over even to mend it. There were many holes on the roof. My mother planted a gourd plant and got its vines on to the roof probably thinking that its big leaves would help covering up some of the holes.

That year we had a big famine. We did not have a single grain of rice. We had few clothes to put on. My mother put several patches of other old clothes in my shirt. Brother's conditions were still pathetic. My father put on an old sweater even in the hot season, because that was the only dress left for him to wear. Surprisingly enough the gourd plant gave us so many gourds. Many of them hung down in to the house from the holey roof. We had had the meals of the gourds every morning and evening for many days and passed the terrible moments of that deadly famine on gourds.

My second brother and I took twenty two gourds to sell at Itahari bazaar. We had thought that we would sell them in three rupees each, but we could not sell even a single one till 4 PM, and then we sold the whole lot in eleven rupees to a hotel keeper and came back home. We had made a very dreamy plan of using those imaginary sixty six rupees from the gourd sale, but we finally negotiated the ambitious plan with an amount six times less than what we had imagined it to be.

That year and for two more consecutive years we suffered from the scarcity of food which lasted at least for two months of every year. My young brothers and sisters too were underfed. I could not endure the situation. Then I told my father, "Baa! I should rather go to work at somebody's house as a cowboy or as a cook. I will continue my studies, after we have a little bit better economic position."

For the first time, I saw my father become so serious and thoughtful. In a deep grim appearance, he slowly shook his head and said, "No, you should not. Once you feel dominated, you can never raise your head. Don't worry. I will manage. You don't have to drop your study."

Then my father took the old traditional plates and dishes inherited from his grandfather's times, old beautifully carved bronze bowls, vessels, water pots and other family antiques to pawn them at Dharan Bazaar and bought rice, oil and cooking stuff for about two months. Just before Dashain, my father, my second brother and I took the only cow to a livestock market. It had stopped giving milk and also had not conceived for the last one and half years. Surprisingly enough the cow did not consent to go to the market. My father slashed it with a stick about half a dozen of times. Finally, we forced it to the market and sold it in two hundred rupees to an Indian cattle dealer. With the money and with a little more money we had, we bought a small he-goat, some rice and spices for Dashain.

Next morning when we got up, we saw in the barn that the same cow had already been there. It had escaped from its new owner's binding rope at night and ran back to our house. The man came to us searching the cow, but the cow did not even get up. He struck it with more slashes to drive it away.

Then, seeing the cow's condition my father promised to pay his money back after the festival. My mother rubbed some local creams on the marks of the slashes on the cow's skin and welcomed it back home. After some months as far as I remember, the cow died in our own barn.

After Dashain, my father pawned a piece of land to a local loan giver, and returned the cattle dealer's money. My exams at the school were to be held in November. My fees were not paid at the school. It was notified that the student who had not paid the school fees would be detained from appearing in the exams. My father had been out for about a month. I told my mother that I would be deprived of taking my exams. Then my mother harvested some rice which was yet to be dry. My mother and I took it in the market, sold it to a merchant in low price and then I paid my school fees. I was tense almost all the year round, and probably therefore, I obtained second position in my class from the first.

During next summer my brothers and I worked hard, irrigated the land seriously on our turns to use the water from the brook-let sleeplessly at nights and also cultivated some extra cultivable pieces of land clearing the bushes aside. We cultivated the nearby barren field and carefully tilled and tended it. We narrowed the gap of food scarcity with hard works. Even then for many years we bought some rice sometimes around the month of Dashain festival.

Chapter Six
The Madhes Rivalries

In Madhes on the one hand we ourselves were in problems, and on the other a kind of rivalry with the tribal lords was always going on. The tribal lords had their complete dominations upon the people in the surrounding villages. Our arrival and settlement in Madhes was not easily tolerable for them in the village. The number of new immigrants was remarkably increasing. In our village most of the new people were either our relatives or from the same localities of the hill sides. There was a common feeling for the common problems, so that there was a kind of like-mindedness in the new people.

Soon we had a good strength to be able to protect ourselves from the animosities of the hostile groups. Even then we suffered from different problems. In those days the tribal lords themselves used to run the dacoit gangs. They had the guns in their possession, and they were inspired and assisted by Indian dacoits. Sometimes they had internal confrontations with other tribal groups. Whoever was more powerful would cause burglary on the house of another in order to shoot, loot and force the other one to leave the village. There were several such real stories of villainy, enmity and murders. Even if we were in the strong positions, we had to uphold the frequent tortures from the thieves sometimes almost in the styles of the dacoit's actions. The thieves were mostly mobilized by those lords, or they used to work in the interest of their lords; though they might be needy poor.

"Who is he? Get up. Somebody is cutting the bamboo bar from the back side. Another seems to dig a hole. See, somebody has climbed up on to the roof and is scratching it out. Who is he?" The inmate would make a sound like.

"Shshsh! Don't shout! Don't make a noise! We will kill you. Hush up." The thieves would point the dazzling rays of a powerful five battery torch light. The thieves were generally with knives, shackles, rods and sticks. There were news items every day that a large number of dacoits tied the house owner, looted everything and attacked villagers with grenade and filling- guns. One of the defending villagers fell dead on the spot and two others were seriously injured.

But the dacoits did not come to our village in that strength. We ourselves used to suffer from famine for about a couple of months every year, but if the food stuff got looted or stolen, the time of food scarcity would be widened and on the fear of the thieves we would leave the village and go away. Therefore, some needy and some projected thieves frequently troubled us.

My father used to sleep with a long and edgy Khukri (a kind of sword) under his cushion. We too would be sleeping with big sticks in our reach. If he heard any type of harsh, breaking, cutting or moving sound around, he would spring up with the weapon and stick, and shout, "Thief! Catch him! Come on boys! Follow him." Then my cousin brothers and we too would shout, scream and run to catch a thief.

If there were real thieves, they would run away with a threat, "We will come back sometimes later." If there was no thief, the movement would be a kind of refreshing and re-energising ourselves from the fear of the thieves. Even then sometimes the thieves would be successful to break the houses and steal away the food stuff, money and other belongings in the state of our deep slumber basically after the midnights.

One evening my father, great uncles, cousin brothers and other villagers caught two thieves red- handed. They were forced to elicit their connections and associations. They went on pointing out their friends and gangs. They told every history of their past records of thieving, stealing and assisting the dacoits' gangs. The villagers grabbed every thief overnight from the surrounding villages. More than a dozen of thieves were collected at a place. The whole night they were given sharp punishments by binding their hands tight on their backs. In the morning when they were being handed over to the police, they begged pardon promising that they would never commit such criminal actions again. Then on the witness of the police, the village committee pardoned them and freed them. From then on in our village there was no such event of any dangerous thief's incident.

After some months early on a spring morning we heard that there was a large dacoit event in a neighbouring village. The leader of the gang fell prey of the villagers' daring actions. The dacoits hurt some villagers, but the villagers pounced upon their leader right when the dacoits were crossing a river. The dacoits had looted all the houses of the village one after another, and that was the third time of the dacoit action in the same village. Then the villagers finally dared to knock down some of them ultimately in a do or die situation.

In curiosity we rushed to see the dacoit's face. He was a strong bodied, tall and puffy faced man of about thirty five. He was firmly bound on a pillar, and a villager was slashing him with a leather whip. The people were trying to disclose his all connections. He was very confidently saying, "We have a strong organization of hundred and fifty committed people. Most of them are from India. They are sharp shooters and skilled archers. They know how to target people from the distance with their arrows out from their bows. You will be killed by my friends. Do you hear that you villagers will be mercilessly killed by my friends? You will not even get to drink a drop of water while being killed."

The villager who had daringly jumped on the robber said that he pressed his head on the muddy water. Then the robber shouted to other robbers for help. They badly charged him with rods in order to free their friend, but they had no time. Other villagers closely followed to help him and finally grabbed the dacoit. There were several severe wounds and cuts on the villager's body. Some local people were putting the herbal creams on his cuts and injuries.

The villagers thrashed the dacoit more and more. There were several marks of slashes on his body too, which were bleeding. He was drenched with blood. On his face there were scars of fresh punches. His face was obviously swelled up with bruises, but he was still threatening the villagers. I could not believe my eyes.

At such beating on him, I thought that he should not threaten the villagers like that. The more he was challenging, the more he was being beaten. I thought, "He too might have had his family, his children and his parents. The children might have gone to school. His parents may be looking over the ways for his going back home. His wife might have had several dreams of life. He too must have thought of becoming a good man in life in his childhood. What made him turn to this rubbish mode? He should not speak like that. The villagers too should stop beating him in that way. They should hand him over to the police soon. The police too might have been tired of the robbery incidents in the villages around. They would beat him more to get him elicited out. Oh, my goodness! What a man he has become in life. If I too became a dacoit in my life, what would happen! People would be beating me so much in the same way! Oh, I can never think of becoming a robber in my life. I must do something good and great deeds."

I had heard that in India there were interesting and dreadful stories of dacoit events. The stories were like: "The dacoits wrote letters and came in the uniform of the police officers. The police personnel that were placed to guard the house saluted them, and later got a call that the house had been robbed. And everybody was surprised. In some places of India the robbers came exactly in the way Solay film was acted, and they performed their actions quite surprisingly."

The robber's threats there too sounded like the threats of the robbers of an Indian film. I was really very much dreaded by his threats, but it sounded dramatically interesting too. The villagers charged him more and more. They actually wanted him to disclose who the robbers' local connections were through whose advice and espionage they came to the village time and again. But he did not tell the secret by all efforts and tortures. It was almost obvious that a kind of ancestral rivalry between the village lords was working. Later in the afternoon, policemen came from a police station which was almost ten kilometres away from the village, and arrested him.

Sometimes later probably after some weeks, another big incident of robbery took place in another neighbouring village. It was on a local merchant's house. But when the robbers started breaking the front door, the merchant slipped out from the back door, and went to a neighbour's house to ask for help and to hide himself. On that night a guest had been there. He was a soldier. The neighbour had an old unused filler gun. The soldier then prepared the bullets from an old zinc pot and came closer to the merchant's house. From the support of a fire furnace of a nearby tea stall, the soldier shot at the robbers. Some of them fell down on the spot and some languished as far as to the field across the river. Some of the clue persons either must have escaped the incident or the robbers themselves carried them away. Altogether eight of them were killed.

The soldier was awarded by the villagers and administration. Thereafter, apart from some minor happenings, the major traditional rivalry-based robbery was almost over in ours and in the neighbouring villages in Madhes.

Chapter Seven
The Oxen Came Back!

My great uncle's oxen were young, strong, fast, well-trained and attractive. That year many oxen dealers asked the price of the pair of the oxen, but the great uncle refused to sell them whatsoever the bid was. That year he was planning to cultivate a little bit more area of land that he had hired on the half amount of crops. Early on a fine spring morning, there was a noise at my great uncle's house. "The oxen have been stolen. Get up. Go to all directions and find them out."

The uncles, neighbours and senior cousins moved to the south and to the west thinking that the oxen could be driven to the livestock market or to the Indian borders. We young boys thought of dropping the school for some days and went to the eastern areas thinking that we would come back round the northern ways. We took some wheat pies, beaten rice, sugar and fried rice with us for the snacks. Towards the bright rays of the morning sun, we crossed Malati plot and towards the midday hailed to Majhuwa, Dhoviyare, Jogiyare, and Drangraha.

A large number of cattle were left on the open field right from the early morning. In today's point of view, it would look like a large landscape as that of a geography channel or a wild Africa in which thousands of wild animals would be grazing in the vast spaces. But those domestic cattle did not have the fear of any tigers, leopards or any hyenas. Over the large plots, we very carefully roved our eyes in a bird's eye view, but we could not have the sight of the oxen that we were looking for. We were really hungry and tired, and near a yogi's hut, we took our snacks. We thought that we would not be able to go farther. We thought that our uncles and senior cousins must have found out the oxen. Then on a garden we started playing a "Catch the Thief" game.

The game was really exciting. By a toss the first thief would be decided, and then whomever the thief touched would be the next thief. It would be really interesting to move from one branch of the tree to another teasing and irritating the thief by singing, shouting and screaming. After a couple of hours, Manoj bro said, "Ok, boys, come on. Let's drop this game. We may have to play other games on our way back home." Then we left the game making funs about the last thief bluffing and bragging about the tricks and skills we took up while playing the game.

"Boys, we cannot swim in the summer when the canal is full and fast flowing. See there is a good amount of water in the motionless canal formed like a pool."

Another elder cousin said, "Let's swim. How many of we can swim? We can play the 'Catch the Thief' game in the water also." Then we decided to stop there. I did not go into the water, because some time ago I had been almost drowned in another place. If Lekraj bro had not pulled me out, I would have been drowned to death. For the whole hour most of us played and some of us kept watching and hooting. The weaker in the tree game turned out to be stronger and cleverer in the water game. While coming back home close to the village, we played another game which was called "Who Crosses the Plot Faster."

The sun had already set. It was almost like a dusk of the darkness. Everybody was waiting for us with some hopeful information. Uncles and senior cousins had come back nervous, tired and frustrated. We too explained that we searched the oxen all around even to the distant villages and landscapes, but we failed to find them out. We said that we asked people if they had seen a pair of oxen of such signs and colours, but nobody gave any positive information.

The uncles were really anxious. They were saying, "Somebody is conspiring against us. Somebody tries to compel us to leave this place. This is a trick to try to displace us from this village. We must be very careful. We must know the person. We must know the reason." We boys too became serious and also guessed that some of the tribal village lords might be trying to dislodge us from the place. They wanted to remain unchallenged masters of their tenants.

Next morning also, our teams disseminated again in search of the lost oxen. We young boys took our ways to the south thinking that we would come round the western ways. In a big plot of land, Baal Krishna bro pointed out to the grazing cattle, "Let's go that way. One ox there looks like that of ours." We went closer to the herds and asked some cow boys if they had seen the oxen of such colours and postures. Nobody said that they had seen any that resembled the kind we described. We talked about the episodes that we had heard of the events of oxen stealing.

Manoj bro told us a story that there was a farmer who had hung the bells on his oxen's throat thinking that if the thief tried to drive away the oxen, he would know it from the sound of the bells. Basically towards the midnights, there would be fears of the roaming of the thieves and of their actions. The farmer kept on listening to the sound of the bells, and he believed that the oxen were there in the barn. At about two p.m., the farmer got up to see the condition of his oxen. Suddenly he was struck with something on his fore head and he fell down. When he got up to see immediately what had happened to him, he realized that his oxen had been stolen hours ago, and a thief was pretending to be shaking the bells in order to make the owner believe that the oxen were there in the barn. When the owner came to the barn, the thief hurt him with the bells and ran away. Then we realized that the thief had hundreds of ways to drive the oxen away.

We moved to several fields and open meadows, but we failed to find out the oxen. Some of the oxen grazing in the distant field looked like that of ours, and we moved to the place, but in vain. From there also we saw some cattle like our oxen but they were slightly different. My second brother suddenly said, "Look! That is our ox." But he was joking by pointing out to a big bull openly left in the herds. The bull was freely and majestically moving in its full arrogance in search of three things: one; a demanding cow, two; another ox or bull that could wrestle with it, and the third is the field of crops into which it can freely crash and destroy. Some of our boys said, "Let's drive this bull to our areas. We don't have any bull for our cows."

"Don't talk nonsense at this time. In their anger, we will be slapped and shooed away by our parents." A cousin thwarted a realistic opinion.

After our snacks we took rest under a tree for about an hour. One of us said, "Let's go to the river down there and take baths and play in the water. It is so hot." Then we went to Budhi River on a half an hour's distance and satisfy ourselves with several games in the water. My brother said, "I have got a ball."

"What ball?" We asked him in curiosity.

He said, "The cloth ball. I have put some old clothes in an old sock and tied it from outside. Let's go to play it on the riverside up there on the ground."

Then we all rapturously ran to the ground and played the cloth ball till it got torn totally apart and went astray. We still wanted to play, but the ball turned useless. To see us still sportive and full of enthusiasm, Baal Krishna bro told us,

"See, it is time now. Let's go to Simarbana. The Simarbana boys must have come to the riverside to play the foot ball. Let's go there and play a friendly match with them."

We went to the football ground on the river-bank near Simarbana village. The boys had just started coming. Then we too were mixed up in the teams and played to our satisfaction. When the sun set, we came back home and reported to the parents and uncles, "We could not find the oxen in all the nearby villages and in grazing grounds around. They must have been taken far away."

Early in the next morning when we were about to disseminate for the oxen search, a man from a nearby village came to talk to our parents and uncles. "See, I have a problem. I had lost my oxen for about a week. I searched them all around. I went even to India following a secret source of information. Finally in a village near Farbisganj, I found my oxen in a man's barn. I inquired about the matter to know who took away my oxen to such a distant place. I came to know that Langru who claims himself to be a so-called village lord sold my oxen to them secretly from the Indian border. He used the Indian thieves to drive away my oxen so far. Please, help me. Your oxen too must have been stolen in the same way."

Then my father, uncles, senior cousins and some other villagers rushed to the nearby village. Langru had just got up. He was in a relaxed mood of the morning in his spacious courtyard complacently walking here and there. My father and uncles greeted him with Namaste, but he just ignored us. Then my father gave a big punch to him. He staggered in surprise. Then my uncles and senior cousins tied his hands firmly on the back, and kicked him. He shouted to his wife to bring out his traditional gun, but helpless he was. Nobody could help him knowing the reason that he had caused Nandu's oxen to be stolen.

We brought him to our village and elicited him out. That probably was the first ever time in his life that he had ever been defied and charged in that way. Nandu said everything in front of us all about the information that he had gathered regarding the stealing of his oxen. After good kicks Langru agreed to bring back Nandu's oxen from India. But he denied to have our oxen stolen. Even then he promised us that if any source connected to Nandu's oxen takers knew about our oxen also, he would bring the information.

After two days he got Nandu's oxen back from a bordering village of India. We continued the search of our oxen in the same way; however we had been almost sure that our oxen too must have been taken away across the border to India by the cross- border elements. Surprisingly enough after three days of the action taken against Langru, early in the morning we too found our oxen comfortably grazing in a nearby field just above the hedges.

Later, we came to know the previous chunk between Langru and Nandu. They were the partners long ago. They had good connections with the Indian thieves and robbers, and they used them as they wished. In course of time an enmity grew between them. Langru got an action of robbery done in Nandu's house once. Langru grew richer, and Nandu's economic condition went down. Finally, Langru wanted to totally finish Nandu economically to turn him to be a farm labourer. Nandu was aware of his situation; however he was growing helpless.

After the oxen scandal, Langru too was exposed to live in a size. My father and uncles along with some villagers threatened him that if any burglary took place in the village, he should be responsible for the connection. His moral was totally down. Thereafter, he was sometimes seen walking around through his paddy field like an innocent gentleman. He appeared so innocent-looking as if he knew nothing about the dark part of life.

Chapter Eight
My Higher Education

After my matriculation, I taught in a newly established village school. My father did not have money to send me to college. He seemed to have thought that I got the basic qualification. I should get stuck to the school job and my young brothers and sisters too should study as much as I did. He looked happy because I got a job in school. My mother and I were unhappy. I had thought that I would study to get my higher degrees, and my mother had a dream that her children should do something good and important in life, so that she would be proud of her womb. More so, she understood my feelings and restlessness.

Next year without the consent of my father, my mother took some loan from a sister- in- law and sent me to college. I left my school job and went to Biratnagar to continue my studies. I met some friends in Biratnagar. They too were full of their boyish fancies and were naturally boisterous in their notions. I thought that I should adjust with some of them as my roommates, and I did.

"Hey, boys! Come on! Come for the meals. Aren't you hungry? What are you doing? Are you reading? Do you just read? Don't I have to read? Do you think my father has sent me money plucking out the notes from the trees? Come on boys. Leave your books now. I too will read together. Ok? Come on." Shiva said to us.

He was in the kitchen for the whole hour cooking meal. It was his turn. We were really hungry and waiting impatiently for Shiva to call us for food. We rushed to the kitchen for the meal, but he laughed at us and pointed out into the kitchen what he had done. He had poured a bucket of water in the fire furnace and got the whole kitchen wet. He had not cooked any meal.

"Oh! My goodness! What have you done, my dear?" I asked him.

He said, "The fire woods were cold and wet. I could not breathe out the air from all capacity of my lungs to flare it up. I failed, and in anger I turned the whole bucket of water upside down in to fire place. Let the fire place go still colder. What does it think about me?"

We were really puzzled. There was no way to continue the cooking. That night we ate some beaten-rice, sugar and gundruk pickle, and slept. About 2 p.m. Shiva woke us up and started cracking jokes. We asked him to sleep, but he went on. He cracked some fantastic jokes about his past life, his relatives and about his fellow villagers. We were bound to laugh. We cackled so loudly that we didn't know that people in other rooms and flats were disturbed. The house owner who lived on the upper floor came down to knock at our door and threatened us that he would tell us to leave his house the other day. We went dead quiet and stifled the cackles and slept off.

Next morning I went to buy some dry fire woods and brought an armful of them from the depot. We cooked the meal together. I was feeling cats and dogs in the stomach. After the meal when I had just finished the washing and cleaning, Shiva shouted from the room that Devendra fell down on the floor. I rushed in to the room and found him trying to get up. But his chin was bleeding. There was a deep cut on his chin. I came to know that he was jokingly trying to put a flying kick on Shiva, but his leg slipped and he fell down.

I tucked up my lungi (a kind of half dhoti) and ran to call a rickshaw from the nearby shopping area in order to take him to the hospital. Some girls of my acquaintances saw me in haste on lungi with a rickshaw. They looked at me curiously as well as sympathetically. In those days to talk to the girls openly would mean quite different. Very few girls used to speak to me.

They might have thought that I was going somewhere else other than to the college. We rushed Devendra to the hospital. The doctor in the emergency put seven stitches and a bandage on his chin, the scar of which is still clearly visible. Some times when I meet him, I feel like asking him, "Is your chin all right?" and sometimes I ask him also. He says, "I was an amateur in those days. I can make better kicks these days."

Shiva was a very good man. He was married at the age of sixteen. He used to go home almost every week some miles away in the countryside from the city of Biratnagar. My house was not also so far from his village. I too used go home along with him in the weekends, but not as frequently as he did.

Being the eldest of a good number of children of my parents, I had lots of responsibilities at home. My mother expected me to come home and help her. I would gather the fire woods for a couple of weeks for her. My second brother and myself would beat the paddy into rice in the long wooden traditional foot-mill with its pestle and mortar at the end which was called dhikki for the period till I would not come back home from my college. From the same lot I too would take some portion to my apartment in Biratnagar.

Once we did not have a single grain of rice, and it was my turn to bring rice for the fortnight. Shiva had gone home and had promised that he would come back on Saturday evening at all cost. Devendra was a moving type of person. We did not know why he would sneak out any time even in the midst of the week. Back at home I told my mother that I should carry some kilograms of rice by all means. My mother said, "Ok, no problem! Spread a shack of paddy in the hot sun, and then beat it in the dikki or you and your brother carry it to the distant rice mill, and make rice as much as you can and then you can take some rice for you. I will help you to move the dhikki if you beat the rice here."

Then, I dried a shack of paddy in the hot sun, and then in the evening my second brother, mother and myself beat the paddy in to rice almost to 40 kilograms of which my mother packed almost fifteen kilograms for me. Early on Sunday morning I put a pack of rice on my back and carried to the bus stand almost five kilometres away from home. I had only as much money as to pay the bus fare.

At Biratnagar bus-park, I asked a rickshaw puller to carry me with the pack of rice to my room. I thought either Shiva or Devendra would be there in the room. I would ask them for one rupee to pay the rickshaw fare. Contrary to my thought, none of them were in the room. The door of the room was locked and unfortunately I did not have the key also. I thought that I should go to another friend's room, and ask him for the rickshaw fare and put the pack in his room itself. There also the friend was not home. Then I went to another person's apartment, but failed to get money for the rickshaw fare. I asked the rickshaw puller to move to one after another place. At every round the rickshaw fare was increasing.

On the way, I met a girl of my acquaintance looking for a rickshaw to go to the market. She shouted to me "Where are you going? Are you leaving the rickshaw around? My mother and I are going to the market, but there is no rickshaw around. Can you leave the rickshaw for us?"

"No, I am in an emergency. I have to go to a relative's house as soon as possible," I said.

She was the girl of my liking. I had a thought in one corner of my mind that I should propose to her for love and marriage some day. But it was my dream only. Had I not been in the difficult situation, I would have definitely made her become slightly thankful to me by leaving her the rickshaw. It was a good chance to develop the story, but my situation did not permit it to happen. She had a few times spoken to me before. Probably she too had some feeling for me. I told the rickshaw puller to pull fast.

I did not tell him why I was making rounds like that. Then I thought that I should tell the rickshaw puller frankly that I failed to get money to pay his fare. I decided to share my rice with him to make up the cost of the fare. He agreed and at a grocer's shop I measured to give him almost three kilograms of rice. Then I carried the pack to the room. Almost half an hour later, Shiva came and opened the key. He asked me, "Why did you bring a small amount of rice?" I did not say anything to his question. I never told anybody how I just moved round in the rickshaw just for a single rupee and how the rickshaw fare rose as high as to the cost of three kilograms of rice.

In Biratnagar in order to maintain my expenses, I went from home to home to give tuitions to the children. To see my pathetic situation and on the request of my mother, Ganesh dai, one of my senior cousins helped me get a job at a contractor's office of municipal taxes. I had to have the night's duty at a road barrier. I would hold the string of the barrier and pull it if any vehicle tried pass through it, and collect the taxes on receipt. All night long I would stay awake on my duty. The places where I had to perform the duty were rough and insecure. At nights some drunken ruffians and hooligans would come, threaten and blackmail me for money.

One night a bit farther from my post, some hooligans forced a shopkeeper to open his shop for drinks. As the shop keeper got late, they started striking forcefully on his shutters with their kicks and punches. As he opened the door, they started beating him badly. His wife and children cried loudly and shouted for help. When the siren of the police patrolling blew from the distance, they ran away.

The policemen came to know who the wranglers were. They searched them around. After the police had gone, one of the hooligans, who was a footballer in the past, came to my post and told me not to tell anybody that he was sleeping inside. The police was spying. After a while the police came and asked me if I had seen the person of a particular name. As I said nothing and looked confused, a police slapped me with a charge that I was hiding one of the hooligans in my post, and went inside and caught the person firmly and dragged him out. But suddenly the person slipped off the police hands and ran away. The police ran after him but failed to catch back the spoilt footballer. At night I watched an informal open athletic competition between the police and an athlete. The police dropped the search thereafter, but next night the man freely came back to my duty post and slapped me twice to have leaked the secret to the police about his being inside the previous night.

After the term of my job at the contractor's office was over, I resumed to the tuitions again. I passed my I.A. Shiva could not get through that year. Devendra had different postings in his job. I had my new friends in my Bachelor's classes. Madan was a voracious reader of literature. Ishwor was very serious, clever, witty and humorous. Uddhav was serious and genius-looking. Govinda was practical as well as professional.

My economic condition was always a hurdle in my education. My brothers too were growing. They expected a lot from me. My mother told me to start a job side by side. Another senior cousin Gokul dai found me a job in the Red Cross Society where I worked in the day time and studied in the morning. The job helped me to complete the first year of my bachelor's level. After a humiliating confrontation with the boss, I was bound to leave the job. Then, Gokul and Manoj brothers got me another job at Anti- tuberculosis Association.

Working in the same way in the day time and studying in the morning, I finished my B.A. After the exams Madan had already left to start a petty contractor's business. Ishwor started studying Law in order to flourish as a lawyer in life. Govinda and I had chanced to be intimate when Uddhav had been to different places on a dancing tour.

Uddhav and I had been really very intimate. It is probably because we shared most of the like-minded feelings and sentiments. We used to talk about studies, love, girls and intimacies. Sometimes we used to talk about philosophy also, and in the end he would ridicule me saying that 'failure in love would turn a man more philosophical.'

When Uddhav too was leaving for home, I turned very emotionally sentimental. I went to see him off at the bus station and expressed my most philosophical notions of friendship, intimacy and the pains of bereavements of the moments of departures. He too expressed the same feelings to me. With a very heavy heart, I said a good bye to him. I felt really bitter, tense and lonely. I wrote a couple of sentimental poems about friendship and departure. I wrote some letters to my friends about the kind of intimacy I felt for them over the time.

Next week on Saturday morning, I was sleeping late. Somebody knocked at the door. I opened to see who the person was. It was Uddhav himself. I exclaimed, "Oh, Uddhav! You came back! Why man? What's the matter?"

He hugged me tight and said, "Yes, I came. We will study further together. Ok?"

Uddhav went to Kathmandu. After some days, I too resigned from my job and went to Kathmandu to do my Master's degree in English.

Kathmandu was very difficult for me; much more difficult than it was in Biratnagar. I continued to work as a tutor to the junior students. My friend Madan sometimes spared some money for me from his business and sent it to me. I was thankful to him but the money occasionally sent by him was not sufficient for me to sustain in an expensive city. Devendra too significantly helped me in the critical days, but I failed to maintain myself. I suffered from Jaundice. At my recovery brother Bharat Pokharel who was a student leader in Biratnagar took me to Nuwakot to work at a school where I finally recovered my health. Back in Kathmandu I completed my M.A. and went to Dharan to work in a University campus as a teacher of English.

In1998 I got transferred to Patan Campus. I had registered my Ph.D. in 1994, but I had lots of difficulties to gear it up. In 2004, I re-registered it, and completed in 2009 under the supervision of Prof. Dr Shreedhar Prasad Lohani who remained a strong source of inspiration in my writings also. Prof. Lohani was the supervisor of my Master's thesis as well as of my Ph.D. dissertation. Therefore, naturally his influence remained always strong in my mind.

Chapter Nine
My One-sided Feelings of Love

Before I moved to Kathmandu I had met a girl in Biratnagar. She was beautiful and brilliant. She used to write fine poems. Quite like half a dozen of times she and I went to recite poems in poetry symposiums. We used to talk about studies and literary creations quite a lot. Amidst the situation I started dreaming about living together with her throughout my life.

Like a grown up boy, it was natural on my part to think in that way. I wanted to express it to her and looked for the ways. After some months of our friendship, I told her that we should publish our stories together. She said to me, "It is nonsense of you to talk like that." By that time I guess that she might have started dreaming about a different sort of man probably more mature, richer, healthier and more attractive than me.

I gave her my autograph to fill with her some intimate words thinking that if something positive came, I would propose to her, but she refused to write anything in my autograph. I gave a pen as a gift to her on her birth day. She threw it down on the floor. In anger I broke the pen into two pieces and threw them farther away. I wished a happy new-year with a greeting card writing that "I wish to live with you forever." She was hostile to receive it and did not show any positive reaction on it. I went to see her at her house but failed to meet her personally. Her father spoke to me in an angry mood, "What is the matter? Why do you come here? Do you have anything to say? Tell me."

I did not say anything to him, but just went away in haste in order to avoid any sort of violence upon me in his angry mood. One afternoon I saw her in the market and followed her. I went close to her and called her. She glanced at me and moved away refusing to talk to me. Then I sent several proposals of love and promises to her by post. There was no response. Thereafter I went to Kathmandu in order to do my Masters in English. From Kathmandu also I wrote several love letters to her, but she answered none of them. Every time I wrote a letter and dropped at the post office as a registered mail, I thought "I should have written more lines; I should have proposed to her with still stronger words; I should have explained the point better; I should have said it in the other way round; I should not have written that line; that expression of mine might create misunderstanding; I should clear my line of whole hearted devotion; therefore I should write another letter immediately to get my feelings more expressed, better explained, and my position better clarified." Then I would write another letter, thereafter another, then again still another. I would send two or three registered letters and one or two by regular mail in a day.

One day, I had only posted the letter when I realized that I should correct some expressions of mine. I immediately went to the post office and asked the officer to give me the letter back telling him that I had to correct some lines. It was a registered letter. The officer said, "By rule it is not possible; however it is not finally despatched to the main post office."

I requested him very much almost like kneeling down to him for his compassion. He gave me the letter back warning me that it was the first and last time that he had ever done for me as an exceptional human compassion. I tore the envelope and changed some lines with more explanation of my feelings that I had thought of, and put it into another envelope, wrote the address and gave it to the post personnel to mark it officially again.

As I had just got out; I thought that I should double check

the address. My letter was being tallied with the previous number. I checked the address. It was right, but I felt like writing an attention on the top of the envelope and I wrote: "If the letter is not delivered to the proper addressee, please send it back to the addressor."

One day I received a letter addressed to me by her by a regular mail. I recognized the hand writing on the envelope and kissed it. I was really happy to receive it thinking that she must have sent a letter of acceptance to my proposal of love. From the time of receiving the letter to the moment of tearing the envelope to read it, I imagined a long panorama of hope in my life and made many good plans to live a happy and creative conjugal life with her. I thought that I should feel a responsible man. But I felt crest-fallen when I opened the envelope. It was my recent letter returned to me which meant a complete refusal.

At that time my frustration knew no bounds. In my giddiness I felt the whole world moving around me as a small ball and I was hanging to fall into the chaos from the swinging earth. The whole world around my life appeared to me completely blank like a big zero. In the extreme feeling of nihilism, I had a suicidal impulse, but I controlled it thinking that I had a big responsibility of my family, and I should not die in a single frustration.

I thought that I should at least sprawl on the road and block the movement of the vehicles. I should call on a strike. I should write many love letters and openly wrap myself with them on my body right from my top to the toe and walk in the streets carelessly, and should let the whole world know that I was in love with my dearest beloved.

I should hang my love letters on the public walls and make the whole world feel responsible about me and convince her to accept my proposals. I thought, "Let the banner news of the national dailies be made by my devoted love affairs, so that she would read the news and accept me."

I seemed to make very swift movements from my Id to Ego and to Super-ego, and again back to Ego and Id. My mind was always filled with her images and reminiscences of those early moments. During the moments of my frustration, one day I was walking along a beautiful barley field with a friend of mine. I was in acute tension internally, but I had not told anybody about my suffering. The friend of mine had guessed that that I had some complications, so that he told me to walk in the fresh air and open environment to renew ourselves from the burdens in mind.

On the way in the barley field we met a man walking alone twitching his back hair sobbing and soliloquizing indistinctly. My friend told me that he was Poet Saru- Bhakta. After going a little far from him, my friend told me, "This man is Bhakta Shrestha by name. He says that he is in love with a girl called Saraswoti. He changed his name as Saru-Bhakta, which would mean a devotee to his beloved Saraswoti. He wrote a book recently which got awarded with a national prize. This man has now a fasting about not speaking to anybody, but to his beloved only. They were good friends previously, but she refused him when he proposed to her. He comes out at night and waits at Tinkune for hours thinking that she would come to meet him. He finds out Saraswoti's symbol number in the exams and goes to sit there before she reaches the exams hall. His whole intention is to meet Saraswoti. Once he was forced out from the exam hall by the guards, but he said that that was not an insult to him, because it was caused to happen by his devotion to Saraswoti."

On hearing such a story about the poet, suddenly I compared

my situation to that of Saru Bhakta and found myself in a vulnerable position. I felt shy within myself and got slightly shrunk. I thought that I would not go to that extreme. I thought that I was a worldly man with all social and family responsibilities. I was the centre of hope of all my brothers and sisters. My parents had a big hope from me. The feeling of responsibility had stopped me from committing suicide at the moments of my extreme frustration.

I wanted to make my beloved, with whom I had such a deep one sided feeling, a happy co-traveller of my life performing all worldly tasks bestowed on me. I had thought that my beloved would be an indispensable companion in my journey of life. Saru Bhakta's situation gave me a slight relief, but by the strike of her sudden refusal to my proposals, I lost hunger and sleep for weeks, and I suffered from a severe jaundice also.

During the same time I came to know that she went to India to continue her studies. I thought that I should not stop proposing to her. I tried to find out her Indian address. I got it and sent a letter again. My illness grew, and the condition of my health went weaker and weaker. Then, I came home from Kathmandu. She too had been to Biratnagar from India. She saw me at the heart of Biratnagar in a crowded road. She came in front me and scolded me badly. She told me in the straightforward way. "Don't expect anything from me when I have already refused your proposals."

I was overwhelmed with the feeling of love for her. I felt like clasping her and kneeling down to her to tell her that I would not live without her. To see her become so angry like the mythical Surparnakha of the Ramayana, I withdrew and concealed my every depth of feeling; however I managed to tell her even in my nervousness that I had recently sent a letter to her address. And, she could send it back to me if she did not like to read it.

In a few days in her absence from her address in India, my registered letter was returned to me by the post marked ABSENT. It was obvious that she still had not reached her station back after the vacation.

After completing my Master's in English, by the suggestion of my mother I went to Dharan, a nearby town from my village. I was appointed as an instructor of English in Mahendra Campus. I had a chance to restructure myself financially. I was able to fulfill the minimum dreams and demands of my parents, brothers and sisters with that job. It was a dignified job too.

From Dharan again I still thought that I should try to win her heart by all means. I passionately wanted to take her in a creative journey of life. Then, I sent some registered letters to her expressing my feelings of deep love and my dream for her to be a sincere and devoted life partner with a view of so many tasks to complete and dreams to fulfill, but I received all my letters back returned by her with the postal marks on the envelopes as, "REFUSED TO TAKE." One of such letters returned to me unread from her tentatively would read like:

Dear R, my dearest beloved!..........!..........!

Please, accept my deep love from every heart-beat of mine and my remembrance from every split of a second right from the core of my mind. I don't forget you even for a second. There is your image every time in front of me whether I am awake or asleep, whether I am at work or at my studies and even whether I am in my consciousness or in my sub-consciousness. You are always surging through my blood and passing through my mind. My life has completely been your domain, your entire kingdom and your whole regime. You occupy all my day, all my night, my every moment, my every time, my breath, my movement, my knowledge, my emotions, my sentiments, my air, my earth and my sky. I feel you in my all perceptions: through sight and smell, and through all my touch, taste and hearing. You are everywhere within me, outside me and all around me. I am writing this letter to you not by a pen, but by the tip of my heart with blood, with tears and with all the best, deepest and holiest of my feelings for you. I don't say that I will give you the temptation of the sky and abyss, pearls and diamonds, dances and discos, mansions and palaces, concerts and carnivals, and of the painless pleasures and riskless prosperity and a very colourful life pattern. I won't show you such dreams. I am a very simple man, very simple with all the worldly ties and compulsions. I don't say that I will lead you always along a wide and straight pitched road. We will have to walk along the narrow foot trails through the thorny bushes up the hill and down the valley and even through the trackless jungles over the boulders and sands, and sometimes also up the well-paved smooth passages and well-pitched roads too, but I say that I will not leave you through all these easy and difficult journeys of life. I don't say that life with me will be always full of bright colours and images glittering and shining, but I say it will be full of brightness and darkness – of all dim, dark and bright pictures of life. I promise that I will be with you through all these colours, images, lights and dimensions. I will be with you through all ups and downs, pains and pleasures and through the states of rags and riches. I will be with you. I will be with you. I will not leave you even for a single moment. Some other persons too might have shown you all the bright pictures of life. If they have, they are false, because life itself is naturally set with variegated images of brightness and darkness, whiteness and blackness, and redness and blueness. 'Life is full of struggles.'

You may think that I am not educationally so much qualified for you. Many more qualified young men might have sent their attractive proposals to you. But I say that the most qualified person for you is the one who loves you the best. This is my claim, and the most devoted lover of yours is nobody other than myself.

You need to have courage and boldness to accept me as your life partner. I have no ambition in life to be rich and great. I think that I should always be worldly, active and interactive. I say that I should never run away from my responsibilities. You know that I am the eldest of the eleven children of my parents. I have to closely assist my parents to rear their children and gear up the family. I don't want my brothers and sisters to be anybody's servants, ploughmen and cowboys. I have to help them grow up, study and work with dignity. To have so many brothers and sisters is not my weakness, but a kind of big strength. If we all eleven children walk together, it will be a kind of rally. People in the streets will watch us with curiosity. If we do some works collectively together, we can finish the work easily and quickly. In this sense, my family is a corporate family in itself. You may think that I have to divide everything among so many brothers and sisters, but the more we all work, the higher the amount of share falls upon me too. The bigger the stronger! Nobody can dare wag their finger upon us. I have to lead all the young productive cream to worthy purposes. More so, I want to walk with a large number of people, friends and relatives together. Can you help me in my campaign, my dearest sweet heart? I believe you can, you dare and you will. I believe you are always bold, beautiful, noble and great. If some other persons say that I should remain away from all these family responsibilities of mine, I will say outright, "Sorry, No!" If somebody wants to seclude me merely for pleasure and prosperity, I will say a big, "NO!" I believe you will understand me and help me in this movement of mine. I believe you will understand me. You will not compel to dissuade me from my responsibilities. I know that you are quite sharp, serious and sensible, and you will seriously think over the matters.

I promise to give you life full of emotions and enthusiasms, love and liveliness, and adventures and associations. Life with me will have risks and responsibilities, troubles and smoothness, and sorrow and happiness. I promise to give you life full of activity, dynamism and cooperation. I will try to give all possible colours and patterns of a simple life style. I believe you will understand me, my situation and my depth of feeling for you, and accept my proposal to be my co- traveller in this very significant journey. Please, try to understand that I have no capacity to bear any more refusals from you, and I also tell you that I probably cannot live without you. Thank you!

-Your most loving, most cherishing and most devoted expectant- R...

When she refused every proposal of mine, I told my problem to a sister. Then I asked her to secretly write a letter to the girl so as to let her deeply know that "I Love her." She too did it as I said. But the girl returned the letter to the sister overwriting on it with a sign pen, "Remind him that I refused him several times before. My thought is like a mountain which cannot be shaken by any tempest." She had written some more and still harsher words, which I don't want to remember here now. My sister handed the disfigured letter to me. I read it and immediately tore it into small pieces and threw them in a fast flowing gutter right away. Some years later, I came to know that she married a foreigner and vanished away from the scene as a non-entity simply for the sake of pleasure.

I had thought that even if she did not marry me, she would not escape from her social and family responsibilities. As far as I knew that there were a large number of people around her who expected a lot from her. She must have hurt their sentiments too.

As I said that I loved her very much, she said that it was my one-sided feeling only. In order to make it two-sided and a successful love story, I made all attempts and promises of the world that I could think and do at that stage of mine. I told her that I loved her more than anybody in the world even than her father and mother. I told her that I loved her from every heart beat and every breath of mine, but she hissed away all the truthful sentiments of mine and went on rejecting every proposal. She gave me no chance for any petition to make her realize that I loved her more than anybody and anything in the world.

The more she refused, the more attempts I made, and the more I failed and the more I was trapped in the complications. Neither could I easily get out, nor could I succeed to soften her heart for me. I failed, and failed and failed. The more I failed, the heavier the blow I felt on me and the more unbearable it turned out to be. My genuine feelings for her got many times broken and many times they were smashed to crust and dust.

I could not go to the height of Saru Bhakta crossing every border and chain of the world. There are still greater devotions of the great men to their beloveds. I remember Dante's devotion to Beatrice, Keats's devotion to Fanny Brawn, Yeats's devotion to Maud Gonne and even Hemingway's devotion to a nurse that were magnificently ideal and great. Laila Majnu's devotion to each other and Romeo and Juliet's sacrifices are frequently talked about as great stories of love. Marx's relation to Jenny and Lenin's relation to Krupskaya are the ideally successful stories. But I am a simple man. I could neither go to the height of Dante, Keats and Yeats, nor to that of Nepali writer Saru Bhakta, nor could I lead my story to the depth of Romeo and Juliet or that of Laila and Majnu. Mine was typically like that of myself with all worldly dreams and desires, wishes and commitments but with lots of pains and sufferings. In the truest sense of the term it was worldly full of emotions, attachments and attractions.

In addition to the best of my feeling for her, I wanted to earn her social dignity and respect. I wanted to establish her at the central position with love, affection and reverence in my big family and in the broad circle of my friends and relatives. I wanted her to create a history of the family together with the offspring through the stream of many generations in future. I wanted her to go together in a long journey of pains and pleasures of a conjugal life. I wanted her to be my best companion to travel round the world. I had thought that I would take her to the village, to the hills and mountains and to the valleys, lakes, jungles, parks, gardens and to the most beautiful parts of nature. We would travel through the rivers, oceans and spaces together. I had thought that I would take her to the fairs, bazaars, and markets and buy her sweets and earrings. I had thought that I would ask her to put on the best costumes over the outing that I could buy for her. I would kiss her in the public places and lift up on my shoulder in front of her parents to show that I would love really, really, really so much. I would express my feelings of love to her in the most powerful words and phrases.

I had thought that we would work for the community services together. We would help the victims and sufferers. We would both work for the benefit of a large number of people. We would try to contribute significantly to the development of a very progressive society. She and I would make our nuptial tie ideal, creative, dynamic and exemplary in the world. But my all wishes failed and all dreams and desires got shattered, when she refused every proposal of mine.

Now I guess the reason why she might have refused me in that way. She must have had a negative impression of my poor economic condition, my large size of the family with so many brothers and sisters, a low reputation of my family in those days, and my weak health. She seemed to believe only in the face values. She never tried to understand my genuine feelings for her, nor did she seem to think in the way that I would easily overcome all those repugnant circumstances in no time. I guess that her mountain of arrogance, selfishness and ambition must have been very strongly fossilized which could not easily be shaken by the gusty tempests of my one-sided feelings; howsoever genuine they were.

In one corner of my mind, I still have some of my most delicate feelings for her, but her body, mind and heart have already been occupied and used up by somebody else for his maximum satisfaction, and I don't have any position in the inner as well outer part of her life. I now realize that her absence for me initially was really intolerable, and now it has become naturally solved by time.

For some years during the moments of my suffering I thought that I should not have met her. But now I feel that my sufferings have been shaped up as catharsis, and all sweet and sour past reminiscences have turned out to be a good creative stock in my mind. The memory of my interaction with her is a little part of the energy of my life. I have neither to glorify her nor to forget her, nor to try to obtain her, and nor to try to damage her. Now without her too, I have almost acquired the state of "Natural selection and the survival of the fittest" in my own surrounding with a large number of friends, relatives and the people in my touch and interaction. I lost her in my life. It was a very unwanted loss; however sometimes I feel that a rocket blasts behind and loses the significant parts, but the blast itself pushes the rocket forward for a much faster movement ahead.

Chapter Ten
How So Soon I Forgot the Blow!

The blow of the refusal was very heavy on me. In the extreme frustration being finally refused, I was just strolling along the pavement of a road in Dharan in a confused mood. Suddenly my eyes fell on two busily working girls in a small hovel. One of the girls looked the age of seventeen or eighteen, and another looked that of fourteen or fifteen. There was no difficulty in guessing that they were two sisters working together in their household matters. It was clearly visible that they were digging mud in the courtyard and making mud-stove in their kitchen.

I was really drawn up to their work. I looked at them for about a minute, but they were not aware of anybody's looks on them. I recognized that the elder one was a girl in my class in the college whom I was then teaching, but I had not had such a concentrating look upon her before, as I did from the roadside that day. I thought that I should marry the elder one with an idea that she was associated with nature and she would cook for me. Then some days later, I myself went to talk to her father and proposed to marry her. I married her in a briefly organized marriage ceremony. I gave a small speech in the wedding.

I have been several times talking about my position in the family that I am the first of the eleven children of my parents. My eighth brother was born when I was twenty three, and the youngest sister was born probably a year before I was married. My wife was really surprised to see so many brothers and sisters of mine, but soon she was so naturally and happily mixed up with them as if she too was born together as one of them. I myself was surprised to see her like that.

One day I peeped into my room through a hole from outside. She was talking to my young brothers and sisters. The small children were asking her if I had bought a house in the city. She said, "No, how could your brother buy a house? He has no money. But one day he says he will buy one."

"Oh, is it that he told us a lie? He is a liar. Wait. When he comes home, I will show him." My youngest brother reacted. On hearing the sweet jargons of the children in the conversation with my newly-wed wife in the room, I could not suppress the laughter. As I laughed loudly, the children came out saying, "You big brother, you are a liar! You are a liar! Wait! I will beat you. I will slash you." The youngest brother ran out to me and started searching a stick to strike at me; I ran away. Other children also ran after me shouting loudly, "You big brother! You are a liar! We will beat you. We will catch you and turn you down. We will kick upon you."

I ran away showing as if I was really scared. It was really a wonderful sport to run away from the children not to let them catch me in "the run and chase game." Later I faced them when I was too tired of running, and I said, "Your sister-in-law does not know it. She is new at our home. I will show our house in the city to you and to her together. Ok?" Then the children and I came home after some more playful activities on the spacious ground of the riverside.

My young and innocent wife was really puzzled to see me in such an embarrassing situation with the children at home. But soon she got accustomed to such a big and sportive family and she said that she found it as a blessing to herself, because she never ever felt bored to live with so many family members together. She enjoyed herself in my big family.

Sometimes when my wife and I came home from my job, she was mostly surrounded by the children right from the way.

They would shout with excitement to her, "Vaudu! Vaudu! Vaudu! See! Our Vaudu has come home." She would then pick up the youngest sister in her hand, and give her fingers to other children to catch and walk together. They would tell her their every story from the time she had heft home.

A ten minute wedding ceremony is continued in a happy conjugal life for more than two decades now without even a single row or a complaint.

Even after my marriage, I had thought I should not divert my attention from my most tormenting beloved whom I loved so much. "I will love her as powerfully and passionately as I did. I will keep her always fresh in my mind. I will remember her in the same strength. Even if she refused me several times, I should remain true to my love and show that my love to her was always true and genuine."

After some days of my marriage I went to my parents-in-law's main house in the village with my newly-wed wife. It was in the countryside some kilometres away from the main road. We did not find the bus to go to the area, because the bus service was not regular on the gravelled road. The buses were not regular. We decided to walk on foot and walked together till late evening. It was a breezy full moon night. Many other people too were walking in the street when they failed to obtain the bus service. My wife and I lifted a bag of gifts and clothes from two sides on its holding ears and walked in the carefree way. On the way I told her some romantic and fantastic stories of fairies, love and marriage, and of the kings, queens, animals, birds, shamans and witches. She too enjoyed listening to the stories very much.

At her maternal house people were waiting for us with delicious meal. Next morning my father-in-law brought me some new dresses to put on. In the day time my mother-in-law took me and my wife to the houses of their relatives and proudly introduced me as her son-in-law. People welcomed us to their houses, congratulated us for marriage and showered upon us with their blessings. They praised the qualities of my wife and said that I was lucky to marry such a good and virtuous lady. We had meals at different houses till we stayed at the village. When we left the parents-in-law's village, we were supposed to come to Dharan directly where I had my job in the campus.

My house was in the village at different location some kilometres down from the high way. I had rented an apartment in the city of Dharan. My mother-in-law packed so many things in various bags and shacks, and got them loaded in an oxen cart. We were placed on the cart as new bride and bride-groom. Many people looked at us from the balcony of their houses and some people came to the roadside to bless us and wish us happiness and successful conjugal life. My wife and I thanked them, paid Namaste of valediction and exchanged waving hands of good bye.

The cart was driven by my uncle-in-law and somebody else. My uncle-in-law had his big radio with him. He switched it on loudly. We were carried in the cart as if a small marriage ceremony of the countryside was being processed. It reminded me of a kind of celebration of the local Tharu community during the fairs. It was really a rare delight in my life with my bride on the oxen drawn cart. The sweet sounding songs from the radio enriched the atmosphere. I looked at my wife's shyly blushing face apparently charmed by the words of the songs and by my company.

I whispered to my wife, "How are you feeling?"

She said, "I feel as if I was in a palanquin with you together."

I too said, "I am feeling as if I am in a chariot with you."

Then I silently promised her that I would never leave her. I didn't know how fast the journey on the oxen drawn cart passed. My uncle-in-law and another person bid a good bye to us at the local bus station of the old high way some kilometres away from my wife's maternal home village.

At the bus park in Dharan, I had to get everything down from the top of the bus to the rickshaws. As the coolies said that they would charge me one hundred and fifty rupees for getting the whole thing down and loading bags and shacks in the rickshaws. That was expensive for me. I had thought that they would charge me only twenty five rupees, but contrary to my thought they bargained for a big amount. Then thinking that I would not surrender to any unusual exploitation on me, I myself went up and gave every pack to my wife and she put them one by one on the rickshaws. It was a rule of the bus park coolies not to let the rickshaw pullers to help the passengers within the bus park for loading and unloading. Then, there came the turn of the potato-shack that I had to drop from the top of the bus. I very carefully tried to push down the shacks on the rickshaw, but the shack of the potatoes burst out, and all the potatoes rolled on the sloppy bus park and scattered all around. Then it took me almost the whole hour to gather the potatoes in the shack again. Many were crushed and many got lost.

After a couple of weeks, we went to Kathmandu for a honeymoon tour. I took my wife to a fellow lecturer's house in Kavre to the east of Kathmandu to have almost like a honeymoon there. On one cold morning in my friend's house, we were all sitting beside a fireplace. I told my friend, "Sir, do you believe that I love my wife more than myself?"

He retorted, "No, I don't believe."

I curiously asked him back, "Why? What's the matter? Why don't you believe? Is there any doubt?"

He said, "Would you please both sit there comfortably cross-legged? I throw two flickers of fire on both of your laps at the same time. Then I will see whose flicker of fire you will throw away first, from your lap first or from your wife's lap! Then I will believe whom you love more; yourself or your wife!"

My goodness! My whole concept of love turned upside down. I had never had the idea from that line of thought. The concept of existentialism flashed in my mind. I had taught the philosophy of existentialism and the literature of the absurd several times before to my students, but I myself had not understood the real meaning of the essence of being and becoming. I understood the whole chunk of existentialist philosophy at a single example.

The fellow lecturer talked about some important ideas. I told him, "Do you know that I left up drinking alcohol around my marriage, and I have not taken even a single drop for the last some weeks?"

He told me that he too had left chewing tobacco in the same way. He told us a story that once he decided to leave chewing tobacco while going to the campus from home. On the way he finally bought a new packet in a shop and took a dose thinking that it would be the final one. He then threw the packet down below a ridge from the road. In the campus, he declared that he left the chewing tobacco forever. On that occasion of making a significant decision in life, he offered tea to the whole team of colleagues and staff. They congratulated him. While coming back home from campus, right on the same spot he felt like watching whether the thrown away packet of chewing tobacco was there or not. It was brightly shining. He then got down and picked it up, and had a dose. Then he threw it two ridges down again.

Back at home he told each and every body that he left the chewing tobacco. Everybody in the family became happy over his bold decision. Next morning when he was going to campus, he saw the packet lying below the road. He then went straight down to pick it up, and emptied it finally. Then he decided not to leave the tobacco in that way. On his way to campus he bought a new packet and thought that he should rather leave it by reducing the frequency of intake slowly and gradually, and leave it finally in course of time.

It was really a wonderful example of neurotic obsession. He practically suggested the method of reducing the neurotic obsession. I too thought that I should not direly leave the drinking. I thought that I should just reduce the frequency in order to leave it. Drinking mild alcohol sometimes and chewing tobacco regularly many times a day are two different things. Sometimes gathering in a convivial atmosphere with friends and relatives with some pegs is not bad, but counting the days and hours of having given up the drinks is another neurotic obsession, that I realized in my life from making a honeymoon visit to my fellow teacher Mr. Ram Sharan Luitel.

Sometimes things really strike in my mind. I was always in the scarcity of money, because I had to bear the expenses of all my big family. After I started teaching English in Mahendra Campus, Dharan, I took a large number of students for tuitions in my apartment. A student used to come to take tuition from me in a group whom I was then teaching George Bernard Shaw's *Arms and the Man.*

In the story of the drama an enemy warrior climbs into the room of a girl and hushes her to remain silent. He has run away to save his life after the defeat of his army. The girl is the daughter of a commander of the victorious army and the beloved of a young officer. As I told the story of the drama to the group, a student asked me to stop there. He wanted to understand whether the door and windows of the girl's room were latched or not. The boy had a logic that it was cold outside and there was gun shooting going on, so that it was impossible for the man to enter the room of carefully guarded Army General's house. More so, it was not at all possible that the windows and doors of the girl' room were left unbolted.

I told the boy, "I can teach you only as much as it is written in the book. Rest either you can guess or the writer himself knows." For three or four days the boy got me stuck to the same point asking me whether the doors and windows of the room were latched from inside or not. When he did not get satisfactory answer from me, he left coming to me for tuition any more. I did not see him in class also. I thought that he must have taken transfer to another college. After five years I met him on the way in the same city. He paid Namaste to me. I asked him, "Hey man! Where are you these days? What level of education have you completed by now?"

"No, sir, I left my studies thereafter. I started working in a press. I am still not so clear whether the doors and windows of the girl's room were bolted from inside or not. You could not satisfy me. Then I left the meaningless study." He said.

I thought, "My goodness! What an obsession does the boy have?" I had no answer. I sent the boy off telling him that we would meet back. I am still curious to know what that trauma-like obsession that is fixed in somebody's mind is. Some problems seem to be permanently entangled in some minds, which may be either put off as great creative solutions in course of time or will still get tougher and tougher to the state of total stiffness never to be easily solved again.

In the coming years we had the children. The wife, the children, my big joint family and my responsibilities made me almost totally forget the idea that I too had deeply loved a girl in my life before my marriage. My wife gave me a good company and courage at every difficult and pleasant moment. She kept my large family skilfully in balance and relieved me from the domestic tensions. With love and veneration, she taught me how a life can be lived smoothly. By her impressive behaviour, she taught me many wonderful lessons of life.

After twenty years when I sat to write my reminiscences, I brought back the girl to my current memory. For a moment I regretted to think how so soon I had forgotten her. I had a guilty conscience over my forgetfulness. Thanks to my memoir writing that reminded me of the sweet and sour moments of my long past!

I would like to make a swift to and fro movement between my past and present upon the striking moments of my life. Sometimes I feel shrunk and startled to get to the thoughts of those moments of my life when they pierce into my mind, and then I feel a kind of revitalization. Thereafter naturally, I start running in the way that I have to do so many things at a time, but I cannot do them all that I have to. Then I whistle with a sigh of relief thinking that I ran a long way up. I have got a limited time and strength. I have to leave the rest of the things to the people coming behind. I fully trust them that they will do much better than I was doing.

Chapter Eleven
I Escaped Death

I have had narrow escapes several times in my life. I remember that I survived by chances only. The natural sequences or some unavoidable circumstances or some extra ordinary coincidences have saved me from meeting an early and untimely death.

In my childhood before we had migrated to Madhes, I got nearly eaten up by a tiger when I went to a teacher's house for tuitions early in the morning. At about 7 a.m. when I was coming back from the teacher's house, people had gathered at a man's barn house. I too went down to see what had happened. A tiger had killed a cow towards the dawn probably when I had passed by the same way while going for the tuitions.

Similarly in one Dashain festival at a temple of Devi, I luckily survived from being chopped apart. Once in Dashain one of my father's sisters said that she would like to sacrifice a young goat in the temple of Devi Dantakali. A team of family members including me went there early in the morning on the Maha Asthami day. There were hundreds of young uncastrated goats to be sacrificed. We waited for the turn. The person that was slaughtering the goats with his edgy sword was almost intoxicated by chopping hundreds of goats' heads asunder. The body of the goat was given to the concerned party where as the head was kept by the priests.

After a long and patient waiting, our turn too came. Our goat too was slaughtered in the same way. The rope that tied the goat was on goat's head thrown to the other side. My cousin told me to bring the rope, for it would be important to tie the body of the cut-up goat. There was no passage to go to the other side. It was too crowded all around. Unconsciously

I happened to jump to the other side through the same place where goats were being slaughtered.

Thinking that another goat had been already placed, the striker frequented his target with his force upon me but surprisingly to say that he stopped his sword slightly before it touched my back. Then everybody was gashed with sorrow, surprise and anger. In anger everybody said that I was saved from being sacrificed. Some angry persons kicked me on my back, some slapped me on my cheeks and some said that the Devi Durga Bhawani spared me. Whatever it was, I remained luckily safe.

I actually did not know how to swim. Near our village there was a river. People had made pools of water by erecting dams for irrigation. The village children used to swim in the river like the fish. They used to swim on the water surface across the currents and also under the surface of the water level. They would play 'Catch the Thief' water games very pleasantly and excitingly. I was really jealous of their charms. I would sit beside the water and watch the exciting events. The boys used to dive from the dam and used to swim through the undercurrent of the water for about half a minute. I had no idea how they managed to float and make movements like that. Sometimes I would think that they would touch the ground by their hands and support their body to move through the water. Those who did not know how to swim would make boats of banana trunks and row through the water. And naturally slowly and gradually they would practice swimming.

I thought that I too should try and play as delightfully as the boy's did. I had a kind of temptation towards swimming. When I said that I too wanted to learn to swim, the boys said, "Come on. You will swallow water once or twice and then naturally you will learn how to swim." I was not still in the mood, but suddenly somebody pulled me into the water and pushed my head down. I used my all energy to come up, but he pushed my head down again. Thereafter, I don't know what happened. One of my cousins searched me out and got me to vomit water. After a while I regained my consciousness.

The boy who had dragged me into the water was Mungre, a boy from another village with a large number of cattle. He used to carry a wooden bat all the time; therefore we would call him Mungre. He had beaten me with his wooden bat earlier on a small quarrel. He was much stronger and a bit older than us. He had developed a kind of enmity with me, so that he probably drew me into the water in order to finish me. My cousins chased him with bamboo sticks. He ran away. From then on he never brought his cattle to our area. Later, we knew that they sold their barns and moved away to other areas. But the memory of my being nearly killed has remained with me almost like a trauma.

When I started teaching in the college, many students came to me for tuitions. One afternoon in a hot season in a large tuition group, a student was about to drink water from a big jug. He suddenly had an unusual sight and he stopped drinking. He made the students aware and threw the jug so violently upon something to avoid a dangerous happening. While about drinking water, he suddenly saw a snake hanging from the wooden ceiling trying to land on my head. It was a very poisonous reptile. If the student had not seen it, the snake would have stung on my head and I would have been dead in less than ten minutes, because it was no where other than on my head. The snake was killed by the students.

One afternoon I was coming home on my motor bike in Kathmandu. I generally used to hum the songs while cycling, biking or even walking. Suddenly a gang fight erupted around me. The boys started throwing spears, arrows, swords, knives and rods. I fell in the middle of their gang fights. A spear passed by my shoulders and a sword struck my mother bike. I did not have time to be scared or dreaded. The only thing that I could think at that time was that I got hit to death, and there was no way out. Everything was so swift that I was not aware of the gangs around in the splits of a second. I tried to escape but it was too late. But luckily the confronting gangs swiftly moved to other direction. And I was saved.

I stopped my motor bike on the road side. Some sympathetic spectators swarmed around me and congratulated me for life. I trembled with fear only when the incident was over. I could not drive my bike due to the loss of confidence. I parked it on the road side and took a bus to my college. I could not take any class that day. Later, in the evening I came with a friend of mine and he drove me home. I asked him to leave the bike at a service centre for servicing. For some days I did not go to resume my bike due to the fear of any sudden mishaps.

I feel that the natural consequences have saved me from the fatal dangers, and I know that the same consequences and coincidences will one day take my life too. I am happy that I got saved from dangers and accidents, but I never think that I have overcome them finally. Writer Thomas Hardy is right to believe that the hostile forces are always playing against us.

Chapter Twelve
To Be a Mother

Once in a subconscious state of my mind I asked my seven year old daughter, "What do you want to be in life, my sweet little daughter: a doctor, an engineer or a nurse or a teacher or a social worker? Lifting her little doll in her hand, she said, "I want to be a mummy." Her answer drew all my attention. My heart overflowed with emotion of love and surprise. Taking her in arms I asked her the same question. She repeated, "I want to be a mummy." I realized that the children speak the truth. Actually mother is the greatest thing to be. Nobody is greater than the mother and nothing is high above her. Once a lady becomes a mother, she feels that she has acquired the highest position in the world.

Mother tongue, mother land, mother earth and mother figure are some of the most dignified terms. Mother's love is so great that it doesn't have any match. Even the animals, birds, insects and all other living creatures have the mother's love probably in the deeper degrees. What is most natural in this earth is the mother's love. The mother often puts her life at risk for her kids. The customs, traditions, cultures, laws and religions which contradict with the mother's love will either be broken or violated.

There are a number of unwilling abortion cases. Some mothers are compelled to abort or commit suicide not because they have any problem of child rearing but because they have the fear of being scandalized about their pre-marital or extramarital relations. I say, they should dare give birth to the children whosoever the father might be.

The mother of a very close friend of mine proudly and openly said that all her children belonged to different fathers.

She might have faced many scandals, denunciations and tortures of the society for her loose character, but later on, her children earned abundant respect for her. She rose to a significant position with all respect.

According to the Greek myth, Gaea (the mother earth) married her own son Uranus (the father sky) from whom she gave birth to three giants, three Cyclopes and thirteen Titans. Cronus, a Titan was married to his own sister Rhea from the association of whom the gods were born. Zeus, the chief god married his own sister Hera from whom many gods and goddesses were born. Then only the generations of gods began, as the myth says.

In the Egyptian mythology, Nut (goddess of the sky) who was married to Re (god of the sun) had secret relations with Geb (god of the earth) and Thoth (lord of divine words). When Re discovered it, he cursed her that she should not have any child in any of the 360 days of the year. Her heart was filled with sorrow for being curtailed from being a mother. She told her problem to Thoth who won some light from the moon and added five more days in the year in which she gave birth to five children and became a mother. Osiris married his sister Isis, and Seth married Nepthys. The son of Osiris and Isis was Horus who defeated Seth in the battle and became the king of Upper and Lower parts of Egypt.

In the Hindu oriental mythology, Kunti was formally married to Pandu; however she had entertained some secret relations with Sun, Yama, Wind and Indra, from whom she gave birth to Karna, Yudhisthira, Bhim and Arjun. She abandoned Karna for some reasons but she remained a proud and loving mother for the other three.

It is said that 'there can be a bad son but there cannot be a bad mother.' Even if the mother scolds, slaps or beats her child, own mother is own mother. She is always kind and caring. Everybody's love except that of the mother's is not fully natural. Other's love is either a friendly attachment or an attraction or a kind of compassion or an infatuation or the feeling of responsibility or a love for own existential surrounding. Even the father may not be able to give true love to his children. Sometimes a woman may conceive from one man and may give birth to her baby for another man to be the father. The real father is either ignorant of the birth or is careless about the number of children of whom he has been the biological father. In spite of all these different types of fathers, the mother is the same.

Everything is obtained or altered except the mother. The mother watches every minute of the growth of her child. She observes and enjoys all activities and movements of her child. The child's pains and sorrows cause her an unbearable shock. To hear about the death of her child is the biggest tragedy in a mother's life. To be a mother is a unique and heavenly experience. Nothing can challenge a mother's love.

Sometimes some women abandon their children or commit suicide thinking that they would be unable to rear them because their husbands died, or deserted them or there were most unbearable reasons. In my opinion they should learn some lessons even from the animals. The mother-animals sometimes keep their kids away due to the fear that the kids would be eaten up by the father-animals. Therefore, the mother has the whole responsibility of the children. For humans, father is an understanding, a social relation, a biological combination and a regular companion for the family co-operation.

Father is a guardian who looks after the family affairs. He guides and instructs the course of the family. But it does not necessarily mean that the father also is equally responsible and caring. That is why there are laws to assure women for property rights and other family rights, whereas males are socially and legally prevented for polygamy, tortures, and other immoral and irresponsible behaviours. Even then the social and legal ties may not go in accordance with the psychological relations, and there can be many hidden tortures and unfulfilled desires, which cannot be easily solved.

The effects of those unsolved relations can be reflected with cold treatments and unfriendliness. If there is no mental and physical association and understanding between each other, the happiness of the conjugal life will go astray. In those situations if the mother does not have anywhere to complain, she should concentrate herself more and more to the care of her children and give a psychological and moral pressure to the husband with all the friendly as well as hostile dealings. In case he does not come to the track and term, the mother has necessarily to have the guts to live separately with the confiscation of her rights in the due way.

A woman has very secret and unexpressed personal constraints and desires. She is more receptive than expressive. She is more possessive than sacrificial. In the feminists' terms, she has the secret pains and pleasures of child bearing, menstruation, sexual relation and so on. A woman's body moves with the lunar calendar, so that she has to face more violence from nature than man does. In this sense she naturally has had different interests and perspectives of life. The family life must be supportive to fulfill most of her desires; otherwise she should try to liberate herself from the artificial bondages.

George Bernard Shaw thinks that woman is the first creation of nature whose self is always active to be looking for a right match for her with the force of her life because she has the sole responsibility of giving a noble birth in the process of creating a superman. In this sense the woman is more child-oriented than to the husband. Naturally she needs freedom as well as care to perform the nature's duty.

It's said that the women in the west have got more freedom than that of the women in the east. They have become free from the burden of child-bearing. But that's not true. Their supremacy has been challenged. They have been deprived of their rights to be mothers. They have been pulled down from their position. There has been a conspiracy upon them. To undertake the family planning measures and give birth to few children according to the need of the generation and the economic size of the family is reasonable but to deprive a woman of being a mother is a big time conspiracy. If a woman does not become a mother, she will have no meaning of her life. I suggest that all women should try to be mothers at all possibility, and enjoy a very respectable position in the society.

In few minutes I thought of many things about a mother's position with my daughter in my lap. She was busy with her own lovely doll in her lap.

Chapter Thirteen
Mummy of Goa

Indian state of Goa has the sea beaches of unparalleled beauty. December and January are the best months to visit Goa. I have been to Goa about half a dozen of times in my life. The first time I went to Goa was when I was just seven. My father took me there. The most suffocating time I remember of my first visit was that I was lost in the train. My father went down to bring some water at a train station on our way back home. The train moved and he could not catch the bogie where I was left. I kept crying for the whole hour and finally he found me back.

The beautiful sea beaches have dragged me to Goa time and again. The most encouraging source for my repeated visit is my father's sister who lives in Goa. She has been there for over five decades. I guess that she and her husband probably went to Goa for their honeymoon. They were attracted to Goa's wonderland, and they decided to live an undisturbed conjugal life there.

They opened a business in the capital town, which is exactly on the bank of the Mandavi River. They gave birth to five children and reared them to their self-standing capacity. After the death of her husband, she took all responsibility of the family and of the business that they had started long ago.

I have got a very high opinion of her. In my judgement she is not an ordinary woman. From an uneducated simple lady of the high hills of Nepal to a well-off business woman of Goa, she must have undergone many troubles, pains and sufferings. Now she has been respected as everybody's "mummy" which she deserves, and also has maintained a position of a mummy of many.

She is a woman of more than 100 kilograms of weight. She cannot walk even about a kilometre on foot; however she travels as far as to Nepal almost every year. She says that she goes to different places on her business connections and spiritual observations. She knows how to use the modern transport facilities to the maximum possibility.

Even at the age of seventy her face is charmingly attractive. A kind of brightness always seems to shine on her face. The luminous halo of the appearance has dominated the clumsiness of the fat body. Nobody can easily face the brightness of her eyes. Amazingly enough she is a very good face-reader. She recognizes the types and qualities of the people simply by face reading. She understands people's nature. Probably it has made her become successful at every step and stage of her life. She is very much careful about her position, her weight and her destination. She thinks much before she does.

To judge the different dimensions of her personality, she sometimes appears to be a politician, sometimes a diplomat, sometimes an astrologer, a psychologist, a devoted mother, a caring sister and, on the whole, a successful woman with many exemplary features.

Recently I visited her along with some relatives and friends of mine. She received us quite naturally as she used to do. She spared herself from her business for some days and took us in her car to different sea beaches, temples, forts, monuments, museums and other worth-visiting places. Wherever we went, there were people to call her 'mummy'. We were surprised to see how wonderfully she has maintained her public relations and business together. She has a big business of the silk items which ordinary people do not have any concern with. The fruit sellers, juice-makers, taxi owners, drivers, receptionists, guards, tailor-masters, boats men, priests and beggars respectfully addressed her with 'Mummy'. She talked to everybody and asked them how they were. It seemed that they all talked with her as their own guardian figure.

My friends were surprised to see her position, her social relation, and her business works. Her personality appeared very influencing to them.

She is a very spiritual woman. She spends her whole morning at worship, prayer and meditation. She believes in charity and kindness. She donates clothes to the poor and orphans. She is a complete blend of spiritual and worldly devotions. At the same time she is equally dedicated to her works and business activities. And, together she believes in God, religion, charity and kindness. She is holy and hearty. She can be a very good example to the millions of women who have not been able to come out of their homes to perform their social and motherly tasks. People need motherly figures at different steps of life, so that they will give up casting evil eyes on women. The mummy of Goa is a living goddess who is a source of love and encouragement to thousands of people like me. I feel like visiting her at least every year on the season.

Chapter Fourteen
The Precipitating Height of an
Ex-Royal Highness

I remember late Dhirendra Shah not because I had any acquaintance with him but because I have seen him at the height of his excessive power. In those days when Dhirendra Shah was a Royal Highness, he exercised the power to the maximum capacity. More than half of the Radio Nepal's prime news was covered by his whereabouts, his eating, sitting, meeting and even sleeping. People who were in touch with him boosted themselves that they were in connection with a mysterious power and they ruled over the people around. Even an ordinary staff commanded a high official on the power of his so-called Royal touch. Dhirendra Shah's associate became millionaire and billionaire overnight. Nobody could resist a small conflict with him. One of the prime ministers turned unfortunate when a small pawn of Dhirendra Shah pulled him down from his post.

The escorting in his visit was amazingly formidable. Once I was walking in a peaceful road in Biratnagar with a preoccupied mind. Suddenly I heard a police siren behind. From the side of the road I watched more than fifty smooth vehicles slip fast. It took me no time to guess that it was no body other than Dhirendra Shah being escorted.

His lion-like movements, his charming youth, his fascinating personality, his wonderful handsomeness, his dominating behaviour and his powerful orders had put him to the submit of many royalties. One day we heard on the radio that Dhirendra Shah resigned from his position and renounced his Royal title. We thought that he would start his career as a good, kind and benevolent citizen devoting himself to the service of the nation.

Luxury begets luxury. He went to live in Britain with a British lady deserting his wife of the Royal position. Frustrated from the heavy disgraces in Nepal, he left almost all his previous connections. Later we came to know that he came to Nepal frequently to see the Royal members and attended some informally organized Royal gatherings.

Once he was charged for instigating some persons to speak against a prime minister. In that case a warrant order was issued against a film actor due to which Dhirendra Shah was forced to go back to Britain.

In the most heinous massacre of the Royal family in the Nepalese Royal Palace, most of the Royal family members including the king and queen were killed. There is no word which can properly express contempt upon the hateful incident. Dhirendra Shah also was shot through in that incident. He had been almost away from Nepalese political scenario. Obviously, there was no reason for him to be killed; however his presence in the Royal gathering was not a mere chance.

After all Dhirendra Shah got killed in the Royal massacre. His funeral procession did not get any Royal treatment, nor did it cover any focused news in the media. The reason was that he was not apparently holding any Royal post. Moreover, his death news was overshadowed by the news of the major royalties.

Dhirendra Shah's untimely demise brought a kind of bitter shock to the world of merry-making. He would have consumed some thousand bottles of splendidly brewed whiskeys, attended a number of well organized parties, reserved some well facilitated hotel rooms, traveled to many beautiful parts of the world and used the most modern privileges intended for the world's aristocrats, if he had lived some more years to his natural death.

Apparently his charming appearance, his wonderfully structured body, amazing fondness and fantastic habits had tempted many. He enjoyed life to the greatest possible extent of amusements. Certainly he was a great man of worldly enjoyment. But his merry-making personality got lost in oblivion.

If he had contributed to the people of the world with his services by establishing scholarships for the underprivileged students, raising funds for the orphans and developing himself as a visionary of life, he would have had a great position in the people's heart, and would have been considered a mini Buddha. I don't know what Dhirendra Shah did for the nation. If anybody is left to remember Dhirendra Shah's soul, I wish he or she would bring out his contributions; otherwise anybody would think that Dhirendra Shah sacrificed the Royal position to free himself for a more luxurious life, and finally died a dog's death.

We remember how people wept at the deaths of Narayan Gopal, Parijat and Ganesh Man Singh: consecutively a great singer, a great female writer and a great freedom fighter of Nepal. People mourned a lot over the sad demise of King Birendra and Queen Aishworya also, not because they were the passing away king and queen, but because they had some sensibility to ordinary people of Nepal. Even the death of an ordinary citizen can be valued much higher than that of Dhirendra Shah.

Dhirendra Shah could not rise above the level of the worldly happiness. Now there is a lesson to many noble births who just would want to enjoy life in luxury, and to those who think that it is an expression of love for the nation simply to attend the escortings and gatherings of some aristocratic powers. Dhirendra Shah is almost totally forgotten now. To the end of his life we had heard that he was growing serious about the nation, but he had no time. His soul might be saying, "Think of the nation when you have time." This is high time for you to give up your luxury for the service of the people.

Chapter Fifteen
A Strange Journey of Life Philosophy

I don't remember the exact days or years, but when I was in the high school, I started thinking seriously about life. "What is life? What is a meaningful life? What can be done to make my life meaningful as well as successful? What are the measures of a successful life? How do different people think about life? What perceptions do the politicians, poets, writers, and the people of some significant enlightenments, achievements and accomplishments have about life? How do they review their life?" Myriads of curiosities were arising in my mind. I had thought that I would one day start collecting the expressions on life from different luminaries and visionaries.

The day I really felt the need of getting something written in my diary was when a very old Norwegian couple – Robert Bergsagar and his wife were leaving for their country after contributing significantly to building a dormitory for the TB patients at the premises of Anti- tuberculosis Association in Biratnagar. I was a staff in the chest clinic and I assisted them for the development of the constructions of the building. They handed over the building to the executive committee of the Association. I was really impressed by their selfless support. They brought money from Norway and spent on the construction of the dormitory which was a big need for the chest clinic in those days.

One day before they left Biratnagar, I talked to them for a couple of hours about them, about their life, their love and their determination for devoting to the help of the people from the church in Norway they were involved in. They too grew emotional and talked to me quite a lot. They probably had thought that I would be the right person to listen to them and tell their stories to others. Then I gave my diary to Mr Robert Bergsagar to write something about the philosophy of life that he had made for himself from the life that he had experienced, viewed, understood and envisioned. He wrote some lines of the Gospel and said that the lines of life of a man are determined by God. That was his perception. And being inspired by his faith in god and his devotion to church, the activities of his life were decided.

Suddenly something flashed in my mind that I should rather continue this journey of collecting the expressions on Life Philosophy. I purchased a good note book size diary and termed it as my "Memory-graph." I seemed to have coined the typical term by myself thinking that it was not the ordinary type of autograph which was in the fashion among the young people in those days. I was proud of the coinage of the term. Then I took my diary to some thoughtful teachers and professors from whom I was really influenced in those days.

Soon I felt that I should meet poets, writers, thinkers and politicians. I thought it was a good idea in the sense that it would be original, typical and more or less unique too. It would definitely give impressions to my friends, relatives and to the persons I meet. I deeply thought, "Who would be the first person whom I should approach for this new experiment in my new diary? Would it be one of my friends or a beautiful girl or a teacher? It was a good idea to go closer to a girl with an excuse of asking for an expression about life. I thought, "By chance if she happened to write in my diary about her intimate feeling for me, what harm was there to continue the relation putting the diary aside? Oh, no! I should not make this diary so cheap."

Then I thought that I should save it from the lovers' market. I should make it a dignified, serious and thought-oriented diary. I should know the grave opinions of the thinkers. I should interact with them and know how they arose to a significant height, and what concepts they have about life, society and about the world. I should know their world view, and understand what the pushing factors are for their rise in life.

The idea of carrying a diary for the collection of the expressions on Life Philosophy gave me some relief from my tense, chaotic and anarchic thoughts. I felt that I was getting some shape, some meaning and some system in my life.

Then with some strange feelings and hesitations, I decided to approach Professor Narendra Chapagain who was considered to be a multiple genius with some good knowledge of language, literature and with some distinct creative potential. Professor Chapagain was in everybody's point a respected figure in those days in Biratnagar.

I had my funny experience with him when I was a new student in Morang Campus. One teacher came and started teaching us the grammar of Nepali language. We discussed some questions with him. When we were not satisfied with his answers, we told him that he should at least read Prof. Narendra Chapagain's book to update himself.

Due to our extreme dissatisfaction upon his teaching, the teacher did not come to our class from next day. Another teacher was placed to teach us the grammar. Later, we came to know that the earlier teacher was nobody other than Professor Narendra Chapagain himself.

After some years in Bachelor's second year again, Prof. Chapagain came to teach us. We were really so happy to have him back. In course of the interaction, later I developed some affinity with him, but whenever I met him, I told him my funny experiences that we had had about him.

He wrote in my diary that it was getting late for me to show my manly works of creativity to the world. He wished me both beauty and intellect in life for my happiness and success. Then I felt really elated and encouraged for more and more collections from the success of getting his expression written in my diary. For some days I showed his expression in my diary to many of my friends. Being excited from the inspiring expression from a popular teacher, I went to some other thoughtful teachers and professors for the expressions. It was wonderful for me to meet the senior intellectuals and hear the stories of their experiences and sufferings through their struggles.

The meetings and interactions with the geniuses made me more and more excited for more visits and collections. On the one hand it was really fabulous to have their own hand written scripts in my diary, and on the other, it was wonderful to listen to their first hand experiences from themselves.

Then I decided to continue it. I met poets, literary writers, politicians, historians and some significant thinkers who had established themselves in the literary and political arena with their distinct traits and contributions. For me these longings for Life Philosophy were not less adventurous than making any expeditions on the mountains. I felt that I was going on some entirely new journeys making some significant explorations and developing a newly creative horizon in life.

Amidst the same time Birat Poets Conference was held in Biratnagar. It fuelled up my enthusiasm about meeting the poets and critics personally and to ask them for the expressions in my diary. Even when the conference was going on, I moved in the hall from one after another poet asking them for some expressions on Life Philosophy. It was really a short time for any writer to think, shape and write about a subject; however most of the poets and critics I asked did not dishearten me.

I got a good amount of collection from some renowned writers and poets among whom were poets like Bashu Shashi, Kisore Pahadi, Khemraj Keshavsharan, Bhawani Ghimire, Govinda Giri Prerana, Upaman Basnet from Sikkim, Kedar Gurung from Dargeeling, Jash Yonjan "Pyasi" from Kharsang, Ganesh Rashik, Tulasi Diwash, famous novelist Dr Dhrubachandra Gautam, famous critic Dr Taranath Sharma, famous Biographist Bashu Rimal "Yatri", and famous dramatist Ashesh Malla, and a very eloquent poet Kedarman Byathit. I met some of them at the conference hall, and some of them in the guest houses. I could not catch famous poets like Madhav Ghimire and Bairagi Kaila, because in the program they were on the stage, and outside they probably were staying beyond my easy reach.

I was about to miss poet Kedarman Byathit also, but his stay was a bit longer in Biratnagar. Prof. Narenrda Chapagain took me to a private residence where I met poet Kedarman Byathit. He was one of the most respected persons throughout the programs, because of his history, age and eloquence. He was a living history of Nepal's democratic movement and was known as a close ally of BP Koirala in his cabinet. No matter how much of philosophical writing he gave me in my diary, it was really a very good time to talk to him. He told us the whole history of democratic and poetic movement of Nepal right from the time of the Rana regime. It was really interesting to hear from him that BP Koirala, king Mahendra and Kedarman Byathit shared some important moments about reading out their poems to one another. He told us that they used to share the books and ideas that they had been reading quite intimately in those honeymoon days of democracy. He said that king Mahendra used to phone them that he wanted to listen to their newly composed poems. It was the king's silent diplomacy to know about the inner strength of the democratic leaders. The same king later confiscated power and put the leaders in the jail cells for many years.

In the Birat Poets Conference although ex-prime minister, leader of the historic democratic movement of 1950/51 (2007 B.S) and story writer Matrika Prasad Koirala was also present as one of the main guests, he was always reserved to tell anything about the historical events and their relations with the kings publicly. In the program Dr Taranath Sharma reminded every body of the felicitation done to poet Lekhnath Poudel during Matrika Prasad Koirala's tenure of premiership. According to him, in the chariot drawing program to poet Lekhnath Poudel, the prime minister himself was in the forefront very actively participating. Everybody praised the premier. On hearing the praises of Matrika Prasad Koirala for his respect to the poet, everybody clapped and applauded him in the conference.

Then Dr Sharma said that he was going back home after taking part in the felicitation, he met old poet Lekhnath Poudel too going home with the support of his stick. Dr Sharma raised a question, "Didn't the prime minister have any mind to drop the poet at his residence in his vehicle at least on the poet's felicitation day?" Then suddenly again everybody clapped and laughed, and some people even whistled in the hall ridiculing the mindlessness of the-then prime minister. From his head up, Matrika Prasad Koirala suddenly very subconsciously made his head down. People laughed to hear the magic of a critic making everybody crest-fallen.

Dr Shrama had earned his fame as a critic by the dramatisation of simultaneous criticisms and appreciations of the writers. He basically charged those writers and poets who were the political leaders also.

The Birat Poets Conference left a deep mark in the literary movement of Nepal. And more so, it was a significant milestone in my life from where I decided to go on with more and more meetings and more collections. I got a good amount of expressions in my diary from the famous creative personalities. I felt I got enriched.

I met Matrika Prasad Koirala sometimes later in his residence and got his expression on Life Philosophy. He had changed his political camp from multiparty democracy to the ruling party-less Panchayat system of king's active leadership. People used to talk about the differences and confrontations between BP Koirala and Matrika Prasad Koirala, the brothers from the same father. Both were the leaders in the democratic movement, both became the prime ministers of Nepal, and both were the literary figures; however BP Koirala reached the summit of the movement of multiparty democracy and died with his own stand. Matrika Prasad Koirala entered the Panchayat system but failed to become the prime minister for the third time.

I had met Matrika Prasad Koirala several times and had had some prolonged talks about cultural, linguistic and literary matters. He never talked about politics with the ordinary people like me. I had attended a couple of talk programmes of BP Koirala in Biratnagar after he came back from India. I regret that I had not started this collection at that time. I had no consciousness about such things in those moments; otherwise I would certainly have asked him to write in my diary with his precious expressions.

Chapter Sixteen
My Encounters with the Politicians

It would be contextual to talk about some of my significant attempts about meeting great leaders for their expressions. I met ex-prime minister and eldest of these many democratic leaders Tanka Prasad Acharya who was said to have established the first political party to fight against the Rana regime and said to be a living martyr. One morning without any appointment I crashed into his gate and requested the inmates that I wanted to meet him. I was taken to his room. It was a cold morning. He was sitting comfortably beside a heater with some members of his family. I explained the cause of trying to meet him, and asked him to write something in my diary from his long and rich experiences as his Life Philosophy.

Without any expression of reluctance he agreed to write some lines in my diary too. Then I asked him some questions from the Nepalese history. He told me some of the traits that he experienced in his life, and he advised me to start involving myself in social service and literary contributions instead of going into the politics. He said, "Politics is not a fair game and you may suffer from frustrations."

He said that the way I was going with the collections of serious expressions about life was the most appropriate way I had chosen. He told me to continue it. I was really surprised to hear such an expression about politics from him. The man who championed in politics in his life himself did not nurse any good attitude about politics. What a surprise!

I met Dr. Dilli Raman Regmi who was known as one of the most renowned politicians of the democratic movements of Nepal and was a close friend to BP Koirala. He was a great historian with his voluminous works in history of Nepal with abundant references and intellectual dispositions. I had a long talk with him basically about his involvement in the democratic movement of Nepal against the Rana regime and his association with BP Koirala. Dr Diili Raman Regmi was said to have professed Gandhi's non-violence in politics, which was his Life Philosophy also. In my diary too, he wrote, "In the system of life the messages of non-violence, truthfulness, morality, celibacy and freedom from family bondages have been delivered to us by the great souls of the ancient times. Great Buddha, Great Jesus Christ, Great Gandhi and many other great saints and souls have inherently delivered the messages in the course of their living. We have these ideals to follow. We have to restructure the human society in accordance with the same ideals" (My translation).

It is a good idea to follow the precepts and styles of those great sages who devoted most of their time to creating the philosophy of life for others for the betterment of all mankind.

Similarly, I visited Ganeshman Singh and C.K. Prasain who rose to a great height basically after the pro-people's democratic movement of 1990 (2046/47 B.S.). Ganeshman Singh had been regarded as the chief commander of the movement and was at the highest level of his popularity. Because of his bad health and extreme constipation, he had to sit for hours in the toilet. He promised me to write in my diary some day, but I failed to get any expressions even at my three visits to him.

At that time when I visited him, CK Prasain another philosopher leader of the democratic movement had been almost totally crippled because of the extreme gout in his hands and legs. He was not able to move his hand to write anything in my diary; however he spent more than three hours to talk to me about history, politics and philosophy. I was really impressed by his talks. At that time he was almost frustrated by the leaders of Nepali Congress basically by the tendency of Girija Prasad Koirala. He expressed his shock not to have been able to meet the top leaders even when there was a program of Nepali Congress Party at Birtamode some meters away from his house. I could easily deduce the sense that the leaders did not visit him even when he was very sick.

I saw that he had saved the tokens of remembrances of the leaders of Neapli Congress with deep love and reverence like: BP Koirala's pen, Subarna Samser's cap and Ganeshman Singh's hand kerchief etc. He talked about Gandhi and politics of India, and remembered the value politics that he wanted to establish in Nepal due to which he was suffering from a kind of isolation even within his party. He too promised me that he would be able to write in my diary some day, but he died after some time before he got finally well. The tragic death of CK Prasain with a large amount of complaints to his own party had a serious meaning with the downfall of Nepali Congress in the Nepalese politics.

In the same course over a period of time I met Manamohan Adhikari, the first communist prime minister of Nepal, Nara Bahadur Karmacharya, the founder of the Communist Party of Nepal (1949), Puspa Kamal Dahal 'Prachanda' the first democratically elected Communist Prime minister of Nepal in the Nepali Republic and the commander of the people's war and chairman of the UCPN (Maoist), Mohan Bikram Singh, a famous political teacher of many big communist leaders, Mohan Baidya 'Kiran' a big thinker of Marxist aesthetics and a widely known hard-liner communist leader of the UCPN (Maoist), and Dr. Baburam Bhattarai, the present communist Prime minister of Nepal for their expressions in my dairy.

Dr. Baburam Bhattarai suddenly came to my place in Dharan sometimes in 1990/1991 on the organization of a public program probably some five years before he went underground for the famous people's war. I grasped the chance to ask him to write the expression of his Life Philosophy in my diary, and he too did not disappoint me even at the compression of time for the programs over the preparation of a revolutionary background in Nepal.

I had met comrade 'Prachanda' in an underground program after the initiation of the people's war in Nepal, but I could not ask him for the expression in my dairy, because he was probably the most searched and most wanted person by the Nepalese security forces, and probably the most curiously wanted person in the international arena. But when he came over-ground leading the peace process and became the prime minister of the republic of Nepal, I met him frequently and asked him to write in my diary, and he finally spared time for some expression on his Life Philosophy, when he had stepped down from the premiership and as far as I recollect, he himself brought my diary to me in a program. I was delighted, and I thanked him.

Over the time through such a peculiar journey, the poets, writers and intellectuals impressed me more than the politicians did. But if the politicians too were good literary personalities, it would be so much the better. The political figures, who lacked in the poetic sensibilities, did not attract me at all. Therefore, I never felt like meeting leaders like Girija Prasad Koirala, Krishna Prasad Bhattarai, and Madhav Nepal who are known as the great political figures in the Nepalese politics with the tenures of prime ministers at different times. They did not slightly tempt me. I wanted to meet Madan Bhandari, a powerful communist leader and a great orator but his untimely death made me feel deeply shocked and my desire to meet him remained unfulfilled forever.

I mentioned earlier that in spite of my meeting with great democratic leaders Ganeshman Singh and CK Prasain, I failed to get my diary filled with their expressions. Not so sensible like that of the poets and other literary writers they were, but the feelings and experiences of their success through some critical struggles in their life, it would be contextual to quote some important figures from the Nepalese history. Tanka Prasad Acharya was said to be the eldest politician who opened a party secretly to fight against the autocratic Rana regime, and later in the introduction of multiparty democracy, he became the prime minister of Nepal. As his Life Philosophy he wrote in my diary, "Be honest with people. Keep up the words. Altruism is very important. Try to gather wealth only as much as you need. If you try to earn more than you require, you will have to encroach into others' territory" (My translation). During the time when I met Tanka Prasad Acharya, he was almost totally silent about politics.

Matrika Prasad Koirala was the commander of the democratic movement of 1949-51 against the Rana regime which succeeded to overthrow the Rana's autocracy, and was the first prime minister of Nepal from the people's families. He wrote in my diary, "Life philosophy has two sides like that of a coin. One type of man lives for others and for the social welfare. The first type of man tries to save others even at the cost of his life. The second type wants to live alone by killing others. I call the first type of man – a man. The second type stands on two legs like a man, but he is no better than a four footed beast" (My translation).

Matrika Prasad Koirala remained silent about Nepalese politics for long and was involved in half a dozen of social organization of people's beneficence. Later, he became active in Panchayat politics but failed to rise up again.

Mana Mohan Adhikari was the first elected communist prime minister of Nepal after the restoration of multiparty system in 1990. He was on exile for many years. He struggled against the Panchayat despotism for political freedom. As his Life Philosophy he has written, "Being a man there are many social responsibilities to fulfill. Man has at least to follow an ideology to guide him. Looking back on my life, I find myself continuously taking an unshaken faith in Marxism. Marxism does not only help people understand life and society but also guides them for the social transformation. The main things are originality and creativity. We have made lots of efforts for the same practices as of today" (My translation).

Likewise, Puspa Kamal Dahal 'Prachanda' was the main leader of the violent people's war of Nepal from 1996 to 2006, and was the first elected revolutionary prime minister of Nepal after the declaration of republic during the peace process. Nepal experienced an enormous bloodshed and turmoil and a large amount of skirmishes, attacks and counter-attacks during the people's war. There were price tags of millions of rupees on Prachanda's head. He was totally underground but actively leading and instructing the people's army and his party CPN (Maoist). I had met him when he was totally underground but it was very risky for me to have his expression in my diary at that time. During the peace process I met him at his residence and asked him to write his expressions on Life Philosophy in spite of his busy schedule. Historically it is really very important to know what opinion he holds about life. He has written, "The extraordinarily positive and purposeful feature of human life, which is the nature's wonderful creation, is the production out of physical and mental labour. From this point of view, the meaning of life is naturally oriented to the ceaseless struggles for the emancipation of labour and the labour force from the world of necessity to the world of liberty. In other words life is the creation of nature that consistently works to change the nature itself. Countless definitions can be given, but it won't be any exaggeration to say that the struggles for Satyam, Shivam, Sundaram (truth, work and beauty) is synonymous to life" (My translation).

Prachanda's transformations appear very slow, and we are afraid that the roles of Prachanda might be over before they take place in the full swing. There are chances for the regressions and counter-revolutions to take place again, because he has erected an edifice on the old foundation itself which is likely to collapse sooner than later.

I would like to present the expressions of Dr. Baburam Bhattarai, another revolutionary leader of CPN (Maoist) who too was extremely underground during the people's war upon whom the Royal government had fixed a price tag of the millions of rupees. After the pro- people democratic movement of 2006 and election of the constituent assembly of 2008, the kingship was overthrown, of which Dr. Bhattarai was one of the main designers. Currently he is the prime minister of Nepal. He is another democratically elected prime minister of Nepal, probably the most popular, most believed by the people, and has to be most responsible for a revolutionary change. From his earliest grades to his Ph.D., it is said that he has never stood second in education, and is now the first man in Nepal's government too. But the foundation he laid and the building he is trying to erect are differently structured. Therefore, there is a possibility of his failure too.

Dr. Bhattarai was in the party programs across the country, and had been to Dharan and to my residence on an orientation in 1990/1991 almost five years before the initiation of the people's war. He was the chairman of the United People's

Front which later was merged in CPN (Maoist) and he headed the Revolutionary People's Council, the people's government during the war. I had stolen some moments with him in order to get his expression written in my diary in 1991 itself. The expression sounds all time contextual for the changes. He wrote, "Actually people have defined life and the world in the way they have wanted it to be, but the parameters of this definition is to decide whether the definition is useful to change life and the world or not. We have to explore the meaning of life according to our experiences of the development from the ancient savages to the struggles of the civilized and productive man of today. The man who finds his place to make a consciously active participation in the historical flow of the human's development is considered to be successful; otherwise life is nothing other than waiting for the time of death. Awaiting death certainly is not life. Therefore, let's find our place to work in the development where there is the real meaning of life" (My translation).

It is really interesting to read the expressions of heroes and leaders of the movements, but what about the king makers? A main builder of the heroes of the communist revolution in Nepal, Marxist theorist and aesthetician Mohan Baidya 'Kiran' can sound still more vibrant and interesting in his expression. He says, "Human life is the combination of physical and emotional elements. Life is an aggregate of knowledge, desires and feelings. Life is full of struggles. It is good to perceive life as the unity of sorrow and happiness, tears and smiles, love and hatred, hope and despair, and comfort and dreadfulness. Life is not meant simply to live but to do something significant. To live really like a man, a wide idealistic view is necessary, and for the attainment of that idealism, man has to consistently involve in activity. Life fully guided by the desire of personal welfare and selfishness is not the real life. The meaningfulness of life is inseparably connected with the struggles for the collective beneficence, country and the people's service" (My translation).

In the mid and late eighties, there was a violent fight of Gorkha Land going on in Darjeeling area in India for an autonomous territory. Subash Ghising, a literary figure was the chief leader of the movement. The war had just landed to the peace talks, and Subash Ghising's residence was intensively guarded by the Central Reserved Police force of India. My friend and I were on a tour to Darjeeling, and suddenly the idea of meeting Subash Ghising cropped up in our minds. We asked the security forces to let us go to Ghising's residence, and crossing the tight security when we reached the place, leader Subash Ghising declined our request of meeting him. As we explained that we were the lecturers of literature from Tribhuvan University, and we would like to talk to him about his literary contributions, he became ready to entertain us. In spite of his very busy schedule, he talked to us for about an hour. In the beginning he had told us about his limitations that he would not talk about politics, but when the talks went on, surprisingly enough he spoke about politics of Gorkha Land movement most of the time. When I asked him to write some expressions on his Life Philosophy in my diary, on the spot he wrote, "I am born here without any borders. O, borders don't stop me" (My translation).

Chapter Seventeen
With Poets, Writers and Philosophers

The strange journey of chasing great persons for their expressions on Life Philosophy in my diary had a mixture of both pains and pleasures with me. I tried to meet Sir Edmund Hillary, the first expeditor of Mount Everest from New Zealand who had climbed up to the highest peak of the world along with Tenzing Norgay Sherpa of Nepal. When I tried to meet him, Sir Hillary was the ambassador of New Zealand to Nepal and India. He was frequently visiting Everest base area where he himself had run several programs of the people's beneficence. I tried to catch him in Kathmandu several times, but because of the unfavourable sequence I unfortunately always missed him before the world finally lost him physically.

Similarly I tried to capture some moments of Indian self proclaimed god of Hindus Osho Rajneesh in Kathmandu. He was probably the most famous person of the world at that time because of his self proclaimed deity, his powerful philosophical orations and his controversial scandals. I could not approach to him because of heavy crowds and tight securities. I failed.

I failed to collect the expressions from a famous American philosopher Richard Rorty whose programs I attended but had no chance to ask him to write in my dairy. I had a chance to speak in the same program as an ordinary guest where famous Egyptian Marxist thinker of the present world Samir Amin was speaking, but had no time and sequence to ask him for his written expressions in my diary.

Once recently only in 2010, with an appointment I went to Satya Mohan Joshi, a great scholar of Nepali culture, history, language and folk lore for some expressions in my diary. I had a prolonged talk with him. I asked him how it was possible for him to walk all the way up from Patan to Kathmandu and back home almost every day on foot like a young man even at his age of ninety one. He talked to me quite a lot. He said that he would just take the simple Nepali food. He would not do any physical exercise or have any yoga practice, but he would listen to the folk lore; folk music and hum it delightfully in his loneliness. Unravelling the mystery, he claimed that the same music kept him healthy, fresh, hopeful and energetic.

He sang some Nepali folk-lore to me and explained the power in their sensibility and musicality. He talked a lot about the history of different places and races which made me sufficiently enlightened and delighted. But when I asked him to write his historically invaluable words of Life Philosophy in my diary, he refused it. He said that he would not be able to shape all those things in a few words. He told me to come to him for talks time and again, but not ask for any powerful written expressions. I felt slightly bad, but concealed the feeling of despair from my facial expression. The meeting was really fruitful for knowledge sake but my mission of getting his expression on Life Philosophy written in my diary failed.

Some of these striking moments that I could capture during this journey can be important and interesting to my readers for the glimpses and to me to engage myself in the panorama of the reminiscences. One of such moments was that I came to know that popular novelist Parijaat was in Biratnagar for some days. I asked Bharat Pokharel, one of my seniors by relation and then a student leader to take me to writer Parijaat and introduce me to her. He took me to a residence in the staff quarters of Rughupati Jute Mills premises where she was staying with some of her relatives.

The meeting with Parijaat didi was really cordial and friendly. She welcomed us warmly. Bharat Pokharel and

Parijaat were well acquainted with each other. I was really curious to know much about her personal life and the sources of inspiration to her writing. She very frankly and intimately told us stories from her childhood to that stage of her life. She was handicapped physically; however her sensibilities were so powerful that she used to write with the internal energy of her life even with a feeble hand. Her powerful and thought-provoking talks impressed me much. Then I asked her to write her philosophy of life in my dairy. She happily accepted my request and cursorily went through the writings of others, and she wrote, "I am not the one to shoot upon the armless people in 'Jaliyanwala Bag.' My history is not tarnished with such charges. I need the meaning of all deaths and murders" (My translation). Novelist Parijaat was then professing a progressive revolutionary ideology, and her writing meant for the need of a powerful resistance movement against all such meaningless killings.

I met famous novelist Lain Singh Wangdel and poet Madhav Ghmire in the-then Royal Nepal Academy. Wangdel was the chancellor and Ghimire the vice chancellor of the Academy. As I was talking to chancellor Wangdel, vice chancellor Ghimire suddenly got into the room for a small counselling. Wangdel told Ghimire not to disturb him, because he said that he was talking to a young man of new generation who would be a good messenger of their ideas to newer generations. He also advised poet Ghimire to entertain the young and serious people. I had long talks with both of them. Wangdel wrote, "Man's life is very short. There are few people who live about hundred years. Time is flying fast. If somebody thinks in this way to desire to do something important and to leave something immortal in this world, and works hard regularly at least for one hour in twenty four hours sincerely utilizing thirty hours of a month and 360 hours of a year, he or she will definitely produce a number of volumes of good books. But the rule of regularity must be followed. I have written some books and have been writing too. I have a desire to write some more. I suppose that I have followed the idea of sincerity to some extent. If the youths follow this suggestion, I believe that they will create many significant literary works" (My translation).

Immediately thereafter, I met national poet Madhav Ghimire in his compartment. Poet Ghimire too entertained me with sufficient time. He told me to leave the diary for that day. I collected it the following day. As his Life Philosophy he wrote, "I have written two lines in a song. 'There certainly will be the moments of sorrow and happiness. Man's life is the mixture of sun and shadow.' You can take this idea as my Life Philosophy. The rainbow-like beauty of the same happiness and sorrow, dream and reality, and knowledge and ignorance is the real achievement of life. 'That can be the darkness of death or the brightness of life. Whatsoever it is, it is the completeness of beauty" (My translation).

Some of the most important moments I had were with the Poet of the Era Siddhicharan Shrestha in Kathmandu. I was a student of M.A. in English in Tribhuvan University, and had an apartment in the next house of poet Siddhicharan Shrestha. As I went to him to ask for some most memorable expressions on Life Philosophy in my dairy, he was happy. From then on, he called me to his house time and again to talk about the poetic creations. He used to talk about the poems of famous English romantic poets. Quite often he used to talk about great poet Laxmi Prasad Devkota, poet Lekhnath Poudel and dramatist Balkrishna Sama. Sometimes some established and rising poets would leave their manuscripts to him for suggestions. Poet Shrestha would tell me to read out the manuscripts to him. He would listen to the poems with his smoking pipe on, and ask me to repeat some of the lines for his better comprehension. Time and again he used to take me together to the poetic symposiums in Kathmandu.

Almost daily till I stayed in his neighbourhood, he would ask me to go for morning walks with him. He would talk about the writings and events of great creations. For the first time I heard from him about the discussions of those days when great poet Laxmi Prasad Devkota wrote Muna Madan, some poets suggested that Laxmi Prasad Devkota's hands were to be amputated for not letting him create any more work thereafter, because it was such a great writing that poet Devkota should not go for the work of the lower values.

In those days I was really lean and thin due to my weak health. Poet Shrestha always used to tell me about the importance of good health for work, creation and easy living. His expression in my diary too reflects his Life Lhilosophy of the time. He has written, "The achievement of virtue, wealth, sex and emancipation cannot be possible without good health. Healthy body is the symptom of a healthy mind. The sounder the mind and body are, the higher the kind of success one can have in life" (My translation).

Later, when I joined Mahendra Multiple Campus, Dharan as a teacher of English literature in 1987, I felt really easy to be travelling to various places thereafter. I could have sufficient money for travelling. And more so, every journey and meeting for me would be a matter of learning as well as the source of my teaching materials that I could share with my students about my recent knowledge and enriched experiences.

Sometimes I wonder how many people in the world would be meeting the luminaries and visionaries in persons and asking them for the expressions on Life Philosophy! In the beginning I thought that it would be a significant and unique adventure, but later for some years I dropped the idea of collection thinking that it would be futile and time taking. And again in the recent years I realized that I was going upon almost like an untrodden road. Great people have talked about Life Philosophy and they have almost passed their whole time in the contemplations about meanings and directions of a human life and its Life Philosophy, but I guess only a few people might have asked them for such expression on Life. I thought that the work I had started was not bad, and then I decided to continue it.

I accelerated my speed for the collection in the recent years, and only last year in 2010, I got one volume of the selected collections of the last twenty eight years published in a book form. I have decided that I should continue this journey across the world with the leaders of significant movements, visions and creative practices.

I am talking about those meetings only which are multi-dimensional as well as historically, politically and philosophically very significant. One of such important meetings I had started worth mentioning was with Dr. Swami Prapannacharya who is known to be a great scholar of Veda. He comes from a Rai (Kirat) family. He says that his real name was Kale (a derogatory name in the Nepali society) and he was a servant at a house till his age of twenty seven. He used to be generally given a jute shack for cover.

He told me that suddenly something flashed in his mind about his life. And he ran away at night covered with the same shack. He went to Banaras and worked as a servant to teachers and students. He washed pots and dishes and finally started studying from the beginning. He perseveringly continued his studies, and finally came out as a Ph.D. in Veda, the most powerful ancient oriental philosophy. He changed his life style from a Kirat to that of a Brahmin pundit, then that of Sadhu and then rose to the height of a Swami with his numerous books, teachings, parables and complicated explanations. His autobiographical book - ***From an ordinary boy to the guard of the Veda*** is very famous.

Impressed by his teachings and philosophical visions, the king appointed him as a member of Royal council which was always debatable and controversial. Sometimes this Swami used to go to Dharan on a tour to the hills or for his peaceful stay at a friend's house or for the delivery of his sermons. I came to know about his visit and went to meet him. He too entertained me well, because I was introduced to him as a college teacher of famous Mahendra Campus. I had recently completed my master's thesis in the stream of consciousness.

I told him about my studies in human psychology. Then he talked about the human consciousness and its space in the Veda. I liked the idea very much. He very cleverly switched over our talk to other ordinary yogis who had come to meet him. He said that the yogis who left the worldly affairs and families for knowledge and spiritual satisfaction would be experiencing better consciousness than those who gained by studies. He said that the ordinary yogis were much superior to the book readers. In that sense he said that he too was inferior to them because his second hand knowledge overlapped upon his real consciousness. The yogis around him were happy to hear the talks, and in their happiness they probably collected a good amount of alms and donations for the Swami's extensive tours across the continents.

It would be contextual here to quote some of the lines of his expression, "It is wise of one to ask the calumniators and criticizers to live closely in the same premises. They will help us to purify our body and soul. One who is pleased by the hymns and praises and angered by calumny can never be a follower of truth. 'Satyam Shivam Sundaram' is not just and right all the time, because there is a big scarcity of truthful, beautiful and altruistic words. Therefore, it seems to be an imported beauty; not the absolute truth. Words for the people's goodness are really scarce. This idea is psychological as well as practical. True medicines are not sweet. Friendly suggestions too are bitter. These ideas are worth keeping in mind and heart. Beautiful things may not be always useful. Sweet sounding words and polite manners may be full of selfish intentions. It is foolish of one to completely believe in anything without any test; however it does not mean to say that all sweet speeches in depth are full of selfishness. A person whom we call a criticizer may be true. A harsh spoken person should not be offended whatever the level of thinking he has. We should try to prove ourselves true by our conduct and dealings, and should not be hurt by other's words" (My translation).

Similarly recently just in 2010, I met famous writer Madan Mani Dikshit at his age of 88 in his own house. He told us how devoted he turned to reading and writing. He and leader Mohan Bikram Singh are said to be profoundly read philosophers and literary figures. Likewise, only last year I met the founder of the communist party of Nepal, Nara Bahadur Karmacharya at his 88 too.

I recall some of these meetings as the most wonderful moments of my life. Long ago I met famous historian Surya Bikram Gyawali in his residence. He was above 80 years of his age at that time. Pundit Chabilal Pokharel, a prophet and philosopher was 91 when I had had meetings with him.

Leaders Tanka Prasad Acharya, Matrika Prasad Koirala, Mana Mohan Adhikari, Dilli Raman Regmi, Ganeshman Singh, and Kedarman Byathit too were above 75 when I met them. I feel fortunate to have met novelist Parijat, writers Lain Singh Wangdel and Ishwor Baral, poet Guman Singh Chamling, linguist Ballavmani Dahal, Historian Dhundiraj Bhandari, and leader CK Prasain; otherwise I would have been always thinking that I should have met them, because they are no more now. In this sense, I feel that my diary which I have recently published as a book form too is in itself a literary and political history of Nepal as well as of the borders.

Here I would just like to talk how I had some adventures upon a strange region of learning by meetings and collections of the expressions on Life Philosophy. I still want to continue it, but simultaneously I would like to follow the suggestions of my guru Narendra Chapagain at the earliest in my diary where he said that it is getting late for me to come up with my own creative works. I am happy that I have started my own creations only after a foundation of significant meetings and sharing of knowledge with other higher creative personalities.

I have had a certain landing. My adventures through this intellectual arena have certainly inspired me for my own creations. I realize that I have passed through a certain process of maturation and suffering in my life.

Recently just last year, I suddenly had an internet connection with famous British poet J.H. Prynne. I asked him to give his concept about Life Philosophy, and he too sent me a sizable writing of his philosophical vision about life. I would like to quote some of his lines here. He writes, "I believe that there is no universal plan for a good life. Each person makes individual choices within the condition of what is possible during a span of life, and each person can also reach out beyond the currently possible, in the direction of hope and in continuing effort to bring hopes closer to reality. I myself believe that hope is not just for the future, and is not for general desire for happiness or utopia. For me it is concerned with true understanding and small advantage, step by step, in relation to what is real in the world of human life, so as to think and act in accord with one's principles and to keep these principles directed towards a coherent aspiration."

Poet Prynne concludes his long definition of life in a condition, "If such a diverse schedule of beliefs and actions in the shifting course of human life has any coherence, the present brief sketch may indicate both somewhat how is (and has been); and also how far hope will make test of what is actual, and will extend the dialectic which itself struggles to hold these two contrary positions in active work: that to be active, this work should be true to principle and experience as well as grasping the contradiction which gives life to each aspect in terms conversely of the other."

In this writing, I don't mean to quote who wrote what. I have published the diary in the book form, and probably sensible readers will put their comments and reviews forward, but the main purpose of this presentation here is how I accomplished the adventures for the collections of the expression on Life Philosophy. I want to discuss how the moments of approach, meetings and situations remained worth talking about.

It is like a story or a chain of many stories to talk about a long journey relentlessly completed in more than two decades. One can obtain many good degrees or many a million of rupees or cover up thousands of miles in such a long period of time, but I captured good moments of many sensible minds over the time. I just want to share the experiences that I have had from such interactions with the political leaders, philosophers, writers, poets, professors and various kinds of luminaries. Wasn't it a good journey? I experienced how it feels like to be a highly interactive man. I experienced the associations and dissociations of sensibilities in practice. I experienced a number of good stories, good poems and good philosophical thoughts that are still left unwritten. I experienced the most concealed thought of the writers that are yet to be written or never to be written at all.

I met writers like Anada Dev Bhatta, Kamal Mani Dikshit, Ram Lal Adhikari and some rising poets in a two day symposium in Damak and asked them to write their views about life. In such gatherings the writers and poets generally do not have much time to ponder over the given concept; however for me it is good to meet many good thinkers at a certain place in a short time and get their expressions written. Even if I meet a few good people and have some intimate talks, they will definitely be a good achievement too. I have been at such gatherings quite a few times but the ones I attended were wonderfully significant to me.

Meetings with professors like Dr. Durga Prasad Bhandari, Dr. Shreedhar Lohani, Dr. Kamal Prakash Malla, Dr. Abhi Subedi, Prof. Dhruv Narayan Lal and the likes were really very much enlightening. I have frequently talked about the life time impressions of the professors in my writings. Every time I have met the professors individually or collectively, I have felt as if I have read a large number of books in a short time. In this way I made this journey, and at this time I feel that I have to make a longer one rather more rapidly than I did in the past. I know that the way I have chosen is interesting, but embarrassing as well as challenging. Thanks to the inspirers! Thanks more on still a longer journey ahead!

From this journey of mine, I found basically three types

of opinions about life: first, very positive, optimistic and progressive; second, pessimistic and negative, and the third type is of the mid position either with the mixture of both optimistic and pessimistic views or like neither highly positive, nor totally negative. Some of the common features are love, beauty, and struggles. Some people have looked at these human characteristics from the top, where as some others seem to have perceived them as the most complicated states which can rarely be achieved in life. A single human life can achieve a part of them; therefore most part of those things can only be gained by the collective efforts.

Like some anxious people I too think that the most significant achievements and personalities too can be forgotten some day. It is very difficult to collect the historical records and evidences of the past of ten thousand years today. We have recently developed some archaeological methods of excavations and conjectures; however script reading of the distant past has become really vague. The meanings of great achievements and contributions too are not everlasting. Therefore, all the creations and dispositions are important relatively at some periods of history only. Then other generations will do more important work or revise what was done in the past, and for their uniqueness and originality, they will replace the old history and personalities. The great poet of today may not necessarily remain great in all ages.

In this sense the significant personalities that I have met and am meeting will no longer be equally significant. And, my campaign of the journey into the philosophy of life too will have little effect after some years or some decades. The most important thing is that I started the journey. I too might have unconsciously followed some others' footsteps, and unconsciously again I too simply can be like a stone on the pile for an edifice. There too lies my satisfaction, because I know that satisfaction too comes from the relative achievements. Therefore, at this stage of mine if somebody asked me what I would want to be in life, I would say that I would be meeting the heralds of my age and would be collecting the expressions on Life Philosophy from them.

If satisfaction is the most important measure of a meaningful life, I don't think that I have said otherwise, because a great conqueror was once asked by his guru to drop his campaigns of conquering the world and live together in the same hot with him, saying that the satisfaction that he wanted to gain from such a large amount of violence and sacrifice may not be so much meaningful after he would complete it or he may not be able to complete it in his life time. If somebody says that he earned a large amount of land property for him, and if he is asked to scale it in the globe, probably he will be frustrated because his area of land of which he is so proud may not be visible in the map of the world. Even from the context of ever expanding universe and from the measurement of the time in the light years, our whole achievements are simply nothing probably more than many trillions of times more invisible and unrecordable like the smallest microbes that cannot even be examined through a most powerful microscope or a most powerful telescope.

Every human life above the common features with that of other lives has its unique imaginations and sensibilities. I too am guided by these powerful thoughts and emotions of my own life, and I think that my small contribution too, even if that is invisible, is something for the enrichment and empowerment of human contributions in totality. I have gained ample satisfaction from my journey; howsoever insignificant or small it is in the total philosophical development. Anyway, I am not the one who gains satisfaction from the seclusion or solitariness, but I am a man who enjoys intermingling and sharing. Because of being highly interactive and worldly, my strange journey is the most benefitting and befitting to me. This is what I really think about my position in the course of my life.

Chapter Eighteen
The Fights for Freedom

How many times the people of a country have to fight for the restoration of democracy? It would be really interesting to talk about the people who fought for democracy, gained it, lost it again, gained it and are again losing and fighting again for getting it back. Democracy has been something like a magic ball which people of Nepal gain it by a violent revolution and when they turn back handing over to some leaders to maintain it, and immediately they know that they have lost it. Nepali people fought against the autocratic Rana regime and gained multiparty democracy in 1950/51, but in 1961 the king of Nepal seized it, imprisoned the fighters of democracy and imposed the despotic party-less Panchayat system.

In 1990 again, Nepalese people launched a democratic movement and restored the multiparty system, but the leaders could not run it virtuously well and lost it again. In 2006 again, the people massively came down to the street to protest against the dictatorship of the king and forced the king to abdicate, but because of the leaders' lack of far-sightedness they may lose this achievement any time again.

The 1950/51(2007 B.S.) democratic revolution was basically led by the Nepali Congress Party in the support and coordination of all democratic and progressive forces. It had the charismatic leadership of BP Koirala. But the people lost this hard earned democracy in about ten years. BP Koirala lived as long as to 1982, but he could not get the lost democracy back in his life time, nor could he lead another powerful revolution throughout his life.

The democratic movement of 1990 (2046 B.S.) was basically launched with the strength of the-then underground

CPN (ML); however its coverage leadership was Ganeshman Singh. Girija Prasad Koirala who became the prime minister for five times after 1990 (2046 B..S) had publicly announced that the movement should be stopped. On the declaration of the multiparty democracy, he spoke that it was the victory of the king also, and people hooted him out on the open theatre program. The charismatic leadership of 1990 (2046 B.S.) movement was Madan Bhandari, the-then General Secretary of CPN (ML). Madan Bhandari died in an accident early; otherwise he too would have been a mere spectator of the seizure of power by the king.

The real strength of the pro-people's movement of 2006 (2062-63 B.S.) was the CPN (Maoist), and its charismatic leadership was Comrade Prachanda; however the coverage personality was Girija Prasad Koirala. The movement was launched in a strong tie of seven political parties on the basis of twelve point agreement with the support of millions of people. This time again Nepalese leaders have not had the strong position, and there is a continuous growth of people's aversion to the political parties. The parties are losing faith of the people. If again Nepalese people lose this freedom, Comrade Prachanda will be a mere spectator. He won't be able to lead another revolution in his life time, because preparing people for another uprising naturally takes a good amount of time.

The present state of republic is historically very hard earned. People have shed a large amount of tears and blood. Every sensible person was involved in this movement in one way and the other. It has long background too. The making of revolution in Nepalese history has a history of more than hundred years of struggles and sufferings.

I too have experienced some of my most difficult days with this political development. But every time when the Nepalese people have initiated a movement, the character and target of the movement has qualitatively changed. The movement of 1950/51(2007 B.S.) was for the political freedom, whereas the movement of 1990 (2046/47 B.S.) had the sole goal of the re-establishment of multiparty system. Likewise, the powerful and historic pro-people's movement of 2006 (2062/63 B.S.) basically aimed to gain the republic. In this sense this gradual development implies the situation that if we lose this democracy again, naturally the next movement will be aimed for another higher form of democracy. There is no doubt, but the struggle will be closer, sharper and more complicated. It will probably demand the sacrifices of more people than that of all democratic movements of the past.

There are both black clouds and silver lining being seen together. Moreover, there is very little possibility of Comrade Prachanda to be the prime minister of Nepal for the second time, because of his inconsistent, unpredictable and impulsive nature, and all the more there is no possibility of Comrade Prachanda leading another revolution exactly in the way BP Koirala, Madan Bhandari and any other charismatic leaders did not feel like going with any more remarkable initiation next time. If he no longer will lead any revolution, and also does not have the chances to become the executive head of the country anymore and still continues the leadership, what will he be doing? It is sure that he will simply go on serving the interest of those handful and selfish persons. A man who says one thing and does another thing immediately can only befool the people and its party cadres for some more time.

During his two decades of his continuous leadership, he managed to lead the party for such a long time sometimes tilting to one internal faction one time and on the other faction the other time. Coming to the power, he tried to apply the same trick with the neighbouring countries India and China, due to which he was exposed for his over-smartness, and he lost the faith of both sides.

Another flicker of hope is Comrade Mohan Baidya 'Kiran' who has firmly stood for revolutionary changes and has been daringly speaking against the intention of the liquidation of the revolutionary spirit before it reached any logical conclusion. Mohan Baidya too may not be able to lead any revolution because he can neither go deeply into the people, nor can synthesize the situation as good as Prachanda used to do. His revolutionarism too can only be limited to the organization of torch rallies and protest demonstrations. Many other political leaders who have been playing their games for the last several years are looking like the date-expired medicines, but they do not realize it.

Every age demands its own reliable, charismatic, competent and comprehensive leadership for the development of any political movement at its successful height, and the same thing is going to happen in Nepal soon. The new leadership is certainly on the rise, and definitely new modes of political developments are in the bright horizon. The fights for freedom are still on for the achievement of still a higher form of democracy.

Let's see what happens ahead, and who will come to lead the further democratic movements!

Chapter Nineteen
The Rigors

Impressed by some student leaders and friends, I unknowingly got myself involved in the student politics not exactly as a leader but as a simple supporter. After I joined in Mahendra Morang Multiple Campus in Biratnagar for my I.A. (Intermediate of Arts), the political conflict between the Panchayat system and supporters of Multi-party democracy suddenly erupted to mass strikes in schools and colleges in the late 1970s. BP Koirala had come back to Nepal after a long exile and was facing trials of so many charges on him from the Nepalese government. During the same time former Pakistani Prime minister Julfikar Ali Vutto was hanged by the army dictatorship under the rule of Zia-ul-Haq. The students of Nepal too launched a protest demonstration against Vutto's execution in which the police made the lathy charges. Then the students continued the protest movements, and in course of the protest demonstrations, the student movements finally turned into continuous strikes against the Pachayat dictatorship of Nepal. The more the Panchayat government tried to suppress it, the stronger the movement grew. In the protest demonstration, I too lined up in the movements organized by the student organizations.

I did not suffer any police batons or custodies; however my faith in politics grew stronger and stronger. The king declared the referendum for the people to choose between multi-party democracy and a reformed Panchayat system. Like most of my friends I too went for the publicity of the multi-party system. In the referendum, the ruling Panchayat system, though it was said to have been suspended during the period, obtained the higher number of votes. The leaders of the multi-party democracy claimed that it was a fake result from the misuse of power and excessive election rigging. I was really sad to think that the process of historical development in Nepalese politics was trickily blocked once again.

The Panchayat system in the intoxication of victory got madder in the following days. Instead of giving rights to the people with the reformation in the system, it curtailed people's democratic rights in the name of security. The Panchayat government took action against the officials who had supported the multi-party system during the referendum. The unseen elements surrounding the king utilized the chances to be more powerful. The unseen, underground and unconstitutional forces did not only use the political power, but also earned money in as many ways as possible.

Later, the same forces had internal confrontations and they took revenge upon each other by exposing, arresting and confiscating the property of less powerful groups by the more powerful ones. The confrontation resulted into the breakdown of family of the-then Royal Highness Dhirendra Shah and his resignation from the Royal positions. The coldness of the relation was latent for many years which paved way for the Royal massacre in which along with king Birendra, his family, the king's youngest brother Dhirendra Shah and some other royal family members were mercilessly murdered. I will talk about the Royal palace massacre later in the chronological sequence of my writing.

The political parties faced almost like a banned situation even after the referendum. They carried on their activities on different other platforms which too were heavily watched and banned by the Panchayat machineries. The communist parties suffered penetrations and splits. Even then the underground CPN (ML) which also was known as Jhapali group had significantly developed over the time through different village-based activities. The Nepali Congress party had a big hang-over of the defeat in the referendum, even if their leader BP Koirala had accepted the results.

Another strong communist section too was developing through divisions, deviations and revisionism from Fourth Convention through Masal to Mashal. And finally when the storm of democratic movement started blowing in the world, Nepalese political parties too got united and launched a powerful revolution with different actions and demonstrations overtly led by Ganeshman Singh and covertly backed by underground ML leader Madan Bhandari from the front of seven political parties. Similarly, other communist parties too got united as United National People's Movement Coordination Committee. In forty nine days, the Panchayat system collapsed. King Birendra invited the leaders of political parties to the Royal palace and declared the multi-party system in Nepal. There was an agreement between the king and leaders advocating for the multi-party system.

Dissatisfied by the limited achievements of the night time negotiation with the king at the height of the people's movement, the next front of the communist parties denounced it, but thinking that it would be a progressive step to protect the limited achievements, they too played significant roles for the exposition of the bourgeoisie.

I had started teaching at Mahendra Multiple Campus, Dharan from 1987. Besides my teaching, I was actively involved in the professor's activities, and I took part almost in every demonstration of the intellectuals against the Panchayat system. From about 1984, I had been a bit more conscious about these incidents. Previously I was a bit bound in my small temporary jobs and had to have associations with various types of persons working in the social institutions. But when I left my job and went to Kathmandu to study M.A. in English, I was free to involve myself in the students' activities. But still I kept myself always in the safe positions thinking that I had to study and had to earn my living from tuitions. I had to send some money home too for my mother. I did not have much attachment with the student leaders except a few. I knew that every student organization was the sister wing of a political party. And naturally, therefore, I knew very little about the parties and their leaders. Moreover, the party that I was supposed to have been passively supporting was underground. I had heard about Nirmal Lama, Mohan Bikram Singh, Bhakta Bahadur Shrestha, Mohan Baidya and Prachanda. I also slightly knew that Nirmal Lama and Mohan Bikram Singh were divided into two parties. And after some years Bhakta Bahadur, Mohan Baidya and Prachanda split from Mohan Bikram Singh heading the new party consecutively one after another.

After 1990 Ganesh Man Singh, the commander of the people's movement, refused to lead the new government of the new situation on the ground of his weak health, Krishna Prasad Bhattarai, the chairman of the Nepali Congress became the prime minister with the ministers from different parties. Even the king sent his representatives in the new cabinet. The parties that had played roles in the people's movement under the banner of United National People's Movement were either reluctant to join the government or they were not requested for. The major faction under this banner was underground CPN (Mashal) of which Com Prachanda was the General Secretary.

After the success of the 1990 democratic movement, the CPN (Mashal) organized an open political front known as United People's Front under the leadership of Dr. Baburam Bhattarai. The party had a unity with the long separated party of Nirmal Lama called CPN (Fourth Convention) again, and formed CPN (Unity Centre) and kept it still underground. It strengthened the open front with the inclusion of new men from the other party. The same front came to the public organizing many programs with the significant progressive issues and slogans and gained a good popularity.

Amidst the situation the new constitution came out with the mixture of reactions. Some parties heartily supported the constitutions, some others had a critical support for it, and some smaller ones did not support it; however they decided to take part in the political activities and in the parliamentary elections in order to expose the new system for more progressive changes ahead. Mohan Bikram's CPN (Masal) and its National People's Front demanded the election of Constituent Assembly and did not take part in the parliamentary elections. The CPN (ML) became CPN (UML) after its unity with the CPN (Marxist) chaired by Mana Mohan Adhikari. Madan Bhandari, an eloquent and vibrant personality was the General Secretary. UML declared that it had a critical support for the constitution and Dr. Baburam Bhattarai's United People's Front criticised it: however it decided to go to the election to utilize the open situation, to associate itself with the people and to expose the reactionaries and bourgeoisie.

In the general election the same thing happened when Nepali Congress gained majority and formed the government. The CPN (UML) scored seats to secure the position of major opposition, and the United People's Front secured the position of third major party. Girija Prasad Koirala, the leader of Nepali Congress became the Prime Minister of Nepal from the elected parliamentarians. The king remained almost silent as a constitutional king, in spite of still holding an unlimited power in his hand.

During the tenure of Girija Prasad Koirala, Nepal experienced direct misuse of power and positions. The ministers were heavily involved in corruptions, commissions, embezzlements, and in all types of arbitrariness in the name of democracy. GP Koirala did an agreement of Tanakpur (Mahakali River) with India which was not in favour of Nepal. The issue aroused a big sensation in the country and GP Koirala was blamed for holding an anti- national practice. The oppositions came down to the streets for protest demanding the PM's resignation. The issue was raised within the parliament and in the court. The third power in parliament was the United People's Front which actively functioned to raise the issues against all those misconducts and misdeeds of the ruling party.

The court too ambiguously defined that Tanakpur agreement was not in favour of Nepal. Within Nepali Congress party also, there was a rift not exactly on the issue of Tanakpur but on the use of power. Some parliamentarians lobbied for Krishna Prasad Bhattarai who was silently backed by Ganeshman Singh, and the majority favoured GP Koirala. Not shaken by the protest demonstration of the oppositions, GP Koirala's government finally was toppled down due to the internal rifts. But the prime minister declared the mid-term general election. In the next election, the CPN (UML) got the highest number of seats even in the absence of Madan Bhandari. Madan Bhandari was killed in an accident which was suspected as a projected killing by its driver and the conspirators.

Next time the United People's Front boycotted the parliamentary election demanding the election of Constituent Assembly. Not with majority but with the highest number of seats in the parliament, the CPN (UML) formed the new government. The chairman of the CPN (UML) Mana Mohan Adhikari became the prime minister. As the new government had just started doing some popular works, the oppositions tabled a no-confidence motion in the parliament in nine months. Mana Mohan Adhikari had been admitted in the hospital after a helicopter's risky landing in almost like an accident. The ruling party requested the oppositions that the PM will get discharged from the hospital and face the no-confidence motion in the parliament with his answers to the charges, but the oppositions forced the PM to answer the charges from the hospital itself.

Mana Mohan Adhikari did not have the majority. Therefore, his government naturally toppled down. He tried to declare a mid-term election of the parliament, but the court gave its verdict against it. Around the same time probably the United People's Front and CPN (Unity Centre) got their splits into two fronts and two parties. One front was led by Dr. Baburam Bhattarai and another was by Niranjan Govinda Baidya. The underground party that was led by Prachanda later developed itself as CPN (Maoist) which rapidly prepared itself for the famous 'People's War' of Nepal.

After Mana Mohan Adhikari, Nepali Congress leader Sher Bahadur Deuba formed the government. The leaders of the CPN (Maoist) had been secretly training its cadres all through the country for the preparation of a large range of a class struggle in the underground situation. Com. Prachanda and his fellow comrades were clarifying their position to some committed intellectuals, journalists and Rights workers explaining why they were going to initiate a crucial movement. In the ideological schooling with the intellectuals, he said that the next movement may become a prolonged people's war. Everybody should be prepared to receive and face it; howsoever violent it would be like.

After the completion of one round of nation-wide schoolings

and public programs Dr. Baburam Bhattarai tabled a forty point demand list to Deuba government and warned that if the demands were not addressed in fifteen days, the United People's Front would be bound to launch a large uprising. As there was no sign of the address to the demands for more than ten days, the leaders of United People's Front dramatically went underground totally out of the general people's contact. And from February 13, 1996 (From the 1st of Falgun 2052 B.S.) the United People's Front and the CPN (Maoist) initiated the People's War of Nepal. Then for ten consecutive years till 2006 (2062/2063 B.S.) the course of a large scale violence and counter violence overshadowed every political activity of Nepal. All political events from the changes in the government to the bloodiest Royal palace massacre moved around the issues and events of the people's war.

As a conscious intellectual, I watched and witnessed every happening of the turmoil, skirmishes, arrests, disappearances, and murders. My previous relation with the openly active United People's Front was broken when it went underground. The leaders and cadres of the United People's Front and CPN (Maoist) were all genuine, serious, sincere and well-read. Their concerns and worries about Nepal and its people drew attention of the people of Nepal as well as of the world. Their demands addressed the immediate and long pending aspirations of the people.

The loots, corruptions, and the anti-national and anti-people activities of the ruling parties, the inconsistently frequent changes in the government on petty interests and various types of wrong doings, favouritisms and nepotisms of the leaders could not compete the devotions, spirit of sacrifices and commitments of the revolutionaries. The government launched a number of various types of police operations and vigilante mobilizations against the Maoists. In the beginning some ministers declared that they would finish the movement in three months, but it grew when it got people's internal supports and it became more and more powerful. During the same time, the CPM (UML) got divided on Mahakali issue and on the ideological matters regarding how to see the growing movement and looking at the national questions. From both factions of the CPN (UML and ML), the genuine cadres entered the Maoist movement.

In the next election the Nepali Congress party again got the majority. The election was held on a difficult situation. The Maoist boycotted the election, but did not disturb it thinking that they would have to undergo more casualties. In the election, the Nepali Congress party had announced that it would go with the leadership of Krishna Prasad Bhattarai, for Krishna Prasad Bhattarai had been a bit popular during the 1990s in the transitional government, and on the contrary Girija Prasad Koirala had lost his popularity on many cases and issues. Krishna Prasad Bhattarai became the prime minister the second time.

As far as I remember, in this second tenure of Krishna Prasad Bhattarai sixty nine Maoist cadres including leader Danda Pani Neupane and journalist Milan Nepali were arrested from Kathmandu and taken into disappearance. The government did not make them public for many days, but when Krishna Prasad Bhattarai was asked for their whereabouts, he flatly said that they have been already killed. When the prime minister himself claimed for the illegal killing of the people, the police force was encouraged for illegal murders and massacres in the fake encounters. The sequence was continued for long. It was intensified when the Royal army took the charge of the Unified Security Force at the declaration of the State of

Emergency some years later. Krishna Prasad too suffered from the internal conspiracy again and was bound to resign from the post. Finally, Giraja Prasad again took over for still a rigorous rule.

Around the same time the most heinous Royal palace massacre took place. The linear generation of the Kingship of Nepal was finished. The king, queen, and the prince along with some members of the Royal family were murdered besides the family of the-then Royal Highness Gyanendra, the shrewd second brother of the king. It was propagated that prince Dipendra on the shock of a love tragedy killed his father, mother, his youngest uncle Dhirendra and other members of the family, and finally shot himself on his head at a suicidal attempt. All the members including the king and queen were cremated on the same day. Prince Dipendra and his uncle Dhirendra were said to be still alive. Dipendra was declared the king of Nepal even when he was supposed to be in the total coma, but after three days Dipenrda too was declared dead.

People said that if Dipendra had shot every Royal member in that way, he should have been declared as a criminal, not the king. It also showed how the Royal family was above the questionable height in those days. During the Panchayat era before 1990, nobody from the people of Nepal ever dared to look at the king and his kinsmen with his or her head fearlessly up. After the Royal carnage Gyanedra, the second brother of the late king Birendra rose to the throne and Paras Shah, Gyanendra's son with his controversial image was declared as the prince and the heir of the Nepalese monarchy. After some days Dhirendra who had renounced his Royal position long ago too was declared dead, and was supposed to have been cremated without many people's knowledge. A probe committee was formed in the leadership of Speaker Taranath Ranabhat for the investigation of the Royal carnage. It looked like a simple drama when Ranabhat himself explained his investigation report publicly in a journo- meeting.

Prime Minister Girija Prasad Koirala was badly insulted by the Royal army and king's supporters from the time of Royal palace incident. He was compelled to resign when he had a conflict with the army upon its mobilization against the Maoists. GP Koirala wanted to use the army at his will in order to suppress the Maoist revolt. Contrary to his idea, the king wanted to reserve all power in his hand and was playing from the back. He wanted to gain power of the kingship like that of the time before the period of 1990. He was advancing with his all minutely calculated steps.

After GP Koirala resigned, Sher Bahadur Deuba of Nepali Congress Party came to the premiership. The king felt a bit easier with him because of his relations with the king's kinsmen. Deuba announced for the peace talks with the Maoists. The Maoists too sent their three member central team responsibly, but the peace talks failed after about four months when the government denied to fulfill some important political demands and the demand of the Constituent Assembly. When the peace talks broke, the same night the Maoist attacked in the army barracks and head quarters in the western districts of Dang and Syanja capturing a large number of arms and ammunitions. The government immediately could not decide what to do.

King Gyanendra told Deuba to impose the State of Emergency and deploy the army. The government declared the Maoists as the terrorists. Before that Indian government had declared the Nepalese Maoists as terrorists. The Royal army fixed the tags of millions of rupees on the heads of the Maoist leaders and announced it publicly. Other parties supported the State of Emergency, but after nine months when Girija Prasad Koirala told Deuba to lift up the State of Emergency, Deuba broke the Nepali Congress party in order to form Nepali Congress (Democratic), and continued the State of Emergency on the pressure of the Royal army.

In Deuba's tenure during the State of Emergency, poet Krishna Sen Ichchhuk was arrested and secretly killed by the unified force of the Royal army and Nepal police. When it was exposed, the whole positive world showed the concern over the poet's murder.

Deuba government had the responsibility to conduct the general election, but when he failed to do it in the assigned time also, the king dissolved his government and took over every power of the state.

The king then made a mockery of the post of prime minister by publicly announcing for the applications. Persons from high politicians to the pedestrians applied for the post of the prime minister. People criticised king's intention. And finally the king appointed Lokendra Bahadur Chand, a royalist and ex-prime minister as the new prime minister of Nepal. The king gave Chand government two basic responsibilities: holding the election from that of the parliament to the local bodies and conducting peace talks with the Maoists. The Maoists too had been saying that they would not talk to the servants, but to the masters. The king was encouraged to capture the state power slowly and gradually step by step. Chand government was nothing more than the king's puppet.

Believing that the peace talks would be successful, the CPN (Maoist) too sent its most responsible five member team on the leadership of Dr. Baburam Bhattarai for the decisive talks. The Royal army had been unpopular for its indiscriminate actions and random killings during the period. The rebel leaders demanded that the army should not go five kilometres beyond their camps. The peace talks went on, but there were symbols of their failure again. At the severe criticism of Chand government from different royalist corners, the King changed the prime minister.

Surya Bahadur Thapa who had conducted the referendum long ago and got the Panchayat system to win and was supposed to have harmonious relationship with the south block of India was appointed as the successor of Lokendra Bahadur Chand. Thapa was always known as a very shrewd politician. Thapa's intention was to fail the peace process and mercilessly suppress the Maoists.

Sometimes probably around the same period (I forgot the dates), the Indian government arrested Com Kiran and Com Gaurav from different cities of India and kept in the Indian jails. Suresh Ale Magar and Matrika Yadav too were arrested and but they were handed over to the Nepalese Royal security forces. Some eleven Maoist leaders were arrested from the Indian city of Patna by the Indian police and were sent to Indian jails. It was heard that many cadres of CPN (Maoist) were arrested from Indian cities of the border areas, and secretly handed over to the Royal Nepalese army, and they were killed without the general people's knowledge.

After some days even when the peace talks between the government and the Maoist leaders were going on, the Royal army killed thirty seven Maoist cadres in a mid-eastern hill district at Doramba. It gave an apparent signal that the peace talks were almost broken. The leaders handed a protest paper against the killing, but they realized that the peace talks were going to fail since there was no any progress. They also sensed that the government wanted more violence. The government had already been prepared for the merciless suppression of the rebels. Actually, Thapa government also was nothing other than a simple puppet of the king and his Royal army.

Realizing the fact that the Royal army may pounce upon the peace talk team also, the leaders sneaked away safely towards their base areas from a western district where a peace talk was organized on the rebel's demand. Right at that time when the end of the peace talks was declared, the rebels shot two renegade army officers in Kathmandu who were actively and mercilessly involved in the suppressions and killings of the rebels.

Then again, violence and counter violence continued. The rebels had already declared the situation of counter attacks on the head from the back shoulders in the symbolic terms. The rebels too tightened their security closer and closer to Kathmandu valley. They had already captured so many major high ways and district head quarters for a short time. The Royal army did the mass killing. There was a reign of terror from the state, and in answer naturally from the rebels' side too. The army arrested many people and secretly killed them. Sometimes the Royal army itself propagated about the encounters, but they were all fake encounters indeed.

The Maoists too had made hundreds of successful attacks. By that time they had launched their successful attacks on from small police posts to large army camps. They were coming closer to the capital city. The king was almost reduced to the Mayor of the capital.

The parliamentary parties were launching the protest movement against the king's activity and his intention. They were demanding the restoration of dissolved parliament and re-instatement of Deuba government. Their protest movement was limited at Ratna Park area of Kathmandu. The king had given the signal to Sher Bahadur Deupa that his government would be re-instated soon. His party too started some dramatic demonstrations at Jorpati area, away from the heart of the city, and in some weeks Sher Bahadur Deuba was brought back to the post of prime minister but not with the executive power. He too did nothing but supported the operations against the Maoists acting as if he himself was doing everything.

After some time, king Gyanendra imprisoned all political leaders of the parliamentary parties. Some were blocked at their homes as house arrests and some were taken to the barracks and jail cells. The king himself declared to have all power, and in his own chairmanship he formed a cabinet making two old Panchayati ex-prime ministers his vice chairmen. Learning from the bitter lessons, the parliamentary parties lost all their faith in the kingship. They decided to launch a combined movement with the Maoist rebels against the king's hegemony. They secretly signed a 12-point agreement with the Maoists towards the end of 2005.

Then from April 2006, the combined people's movement started. The Royal government imposed curfews regularly for nineteen days in Kathmandu as well as in the major cities of Nepal. The more curfews and more methods of suppression the government undertook, the more people came down to the street. It was probably the largest number of people in the world that came down to the streets for demonstration at a time in Nepal. To say that more than hundred million people on the road across the country violating the curfews was not a joke. Basically in Kathmandu it was really most surprising that they systematically protested and systematically went back home and to their shelters. Later, it was known that the Maoists had brought a large number of people from the rural areas.

As there were some big unrests every time in Nepal, India used to play some roles for mediation. India sent its special envoy Karan Singh and had some understanding with the king, but the Nepalese people did not agree with Karan Singh's solution, and continued the movement. In nineteen days the king finally was bound to restore the long dissolved parliament, and handed over all his power to it. The people had wanted to overthrow the king from the movement, but the parliamentary parties were afraid of the idea that the power might go to the rebels. They secretly negotiated with the king. The rebels sensed a kind of conspiracy against the people's movement again.

The new government in the leadership of Girija Prasad Koirala was formed, but the CPN (Maoist) was excluded. The Maoist protested that the agreement was signed by the parliamentary parties at the height of the movement saying that it was a serious conspiracy against the Nepalese people again. Then when the parliamentary parties promised that a new parliament would be formed along with the Maoists, several rounds of talks between the parties and the Maoists were organized to settle the problems.

A man who was underground for more than thirty years regularly and was the leader of the ten years' violent People War of Nepal too came to Kathmandu in order to hold talks and interfere into the politics for the right sharing of political power. He was the chairman and supreme leader of the CPN (Maoist) known as Puspa Kamal Dahal 'Prachanda. Everybody was curious to see him. Some people had said that Prachanda was nobody other than king Gyanendra himself, and some were saying that Prachanda is just a symbol. They used to say that the real Prachanda had been already killed, and whoever came to the next leadership was named as Prachanda.' Contrary to every body's belief, Prachanda came over-ground with a large number of his supporters and PLA fighters with him and delivered a magnificently eloquent open interview with the press meet at Baluwatar extemporarily. I was not at all curious about his active presence in the underground politics, because I had met him a couple of times before.

Quite like a month before Prachanda came to Kathmandu, the Maiosts had organized a public gathering in Kathamandu in which more than a million of people lashed into the Kathmandu valley which almost disturbed all systems of the Capital city. On the back ground of the strength of the people's war and people's support, Prachanda's bargain on the talk-table appeared always powerful. Even then, when the old political forces did not want to come up forward about sharing the power with the new force, the Maoists launched pressures by taking a large number of cadres to the talk spots generally at Baluwataar outside the prime minister's residence.

The peace treaty was finally signed about the end of the people's war. Then a new parliament was formed. An interim constitution was promulgated. In the power sharing process, the Maoists got eighty four seats in the new parliament. A new government was formed along with the Maoists. The Maoist army (PLA - combatants) were placed at different camps (cantonments) with a significant amount of budget for their logistics and allowances. Their weapons were locked up, and the same amount of the weapons of Nepal army (formerly Royal army) too was supposed to have been locked up.

The UN was on the mediation. The committee on the leadership of the UN went to different camps in order to judge the standard of the People's Liberation Army. Those who did not meet the UN standard were sent back home, but the Maoist party organized them in its different party committees. Later, the UN was forced to leave its role of the mediation of the peace process by other parliamentary parties on the charge of its tilting slightly to the Maoists, but the reality was not like that. Actually it was due to the pressures of some countries which did not want to see the UN's mediation in the peace process of Nepal; the UN finally left its mediation role.

The CPN (Maoist) party raised a Young Communist League (YCL) from semi trained young cadres, and placed them at different locations for social services, developmental activities and justice providing practices. YCL cadres were the real active forces of the over-ground CPN (Maoist) which played a significant role to establish the Maoists in the political arena of Nepal. They provided security to the leaders and helped people to relieve from age-long injustices and dominations. The same force cautiously helped the party to secure the highest number of seats in the Constituent Assembly election by carefully watching upon any possibility of rigging. The YCL tried to establish a virtuous society. They took actions again the professional dons, wranglers and ruffians.

After the Constituent Assembly election, from the first meeting the country was declared republic. The king who was turned almost powerless was forced to leave the throne from the decision of the Constituent Assembly. Comrade Puspa Kamal Dahal 'Prachanda' being the supreme leader of the armed rebels and the chairman of the CPN (Maoist) became the most powerful first prime minister of the Nepalese Republic.

Over the time through the violent conflicts of the people's war, and through the peace process, the party had almost divinized the personality of Comrade Prachanda which had made him arrogant like any arrogant king of mythology. I, as the General Secretary of Nepal University Progressive Teacher's Association (NUPTA), and the President of Nepal National University Teachers' Association (NUTAN) and as a progressive intellectual, went to him several times in order to remind him of the party's commitments and promises to the people, but he never cared the voice of the intellectuals. He just indulged in the praises and supports, and enjoyed road-shows and protest demonstrations by the supporters. He only liked to make public speeches. He was reluctant to perform the premier's duty as a clever statesman. He shattered everybody's hope in nine months.

In nine months of his premiership he did not even move a straw from one place to another. Finally when his conflict with the army chief grew, he tried to curb him out from the post bluntly without following the simple legal and constitutional processes. The president placed back the army chief the same night. Then divinized impulsive Prachanda himself was morally bound to resign from the premiership.

Com Prachanda probably had thought that his resignation would lay pressure on the president and he would be reinstated to the same post. But all the other parties projected Madhav Nepal for the new prime minister, and Prachanda fell flat.

Then the CPN (Maoist) in the spirit of an old rebel force launched several demonstrations against the president Ram Baran Yadav's steps. The party soon changed its old slogan and stance, and demanded Madhav Nepal's resignation from the premiership. Few weeks before the deadline of the term of the Constituent Assembly, it announced an indefinite closure throughout the nation declaring that if Madhav Nepal did not submit the resignation, the party would not go forward to extend the CA term. But in the mid night of the last day, it decided to extend the term of the CA saying that it was a baby born from the womb of the Maoists themselves.

Just before the extension of the CA term, the party organized a meeting with the bourgeois intellectuals and businessmen at a hotel. Comrade Prachanda apologized with them to have troubled them from the Maoist cadres over the years. He clearly spoke to them that there is no conflict of the party with them forgetting the concepts of the everlasting conflict between "the Haves and the Have-nots." The other day he with his fellow comrades moved round the whole ring road of the Kathmandu valley waving hands and bidding good bye to the large number of cadres and supporters that had gathered in Kathmandu valley from different corners of the country in a false hope.

Com Prachanda has been constantly trying to come to the post of prime minister again and again, but the more he tries, the farther the post seems to go. For the success of this practice, currently it is heard that he has developed close links with some foreign secret agencies too.

Another leader Dr. Baburam Bhattarai who was the centre of all hope of the Nepalese people had set some good records and images when he was the finance minister during Prachanda's tenure. Recently at the support of some parties and millions of people, he rose to the post of the prime minister of Nepal, but he too seems to have lost the people's confidence after his India visit which remained mostly debatable within his party and set a controversial record in his career. Violating his previous good records, he formed a largest cabinet in the history of Nepal which shows that his premiership too currently has no future.

Besides working in the University, over the last more than twenty years, I sometimes worked at the intellectual's front, sometimes at the Rights organization and sometimes as an editor of some magazines during the period of conflicts and through the peace process advocating that the Maoists were only genuine political force in Nepal who are guided by an ideology. For my opinions and stance, I too suffered lots of threats and tortures like many other intellectual colleagues, journalists and writers too did.

Being an intellectual, I deeply watched every situation closely as a supporter of the radiant sacrifices and jubilant activities of the revolutionaries in the democratic movements. From 1996 to 2006, I also watched and witnessed how the government imposed Kilo- sera 2, and killed several hundred people in the simple suspicion of their being the rebels. Likewise, I watched the Cordon, Search and Kill Operation of the Royal army in which a mass killings and disappearances of the people were done. I also watched the most dreadful sufferings and bearings of the people: the killings and disappearances of thousands of most wonderful sons and daughters of the Nepali People. I also watched how the Maoists too sometimes in their excitement lost their wisdom and killed the police, army and detectives just because they belonged to the enemy camps. The innocent people suffered a lot being squeezed between the conflicting forces.

But when peace process began, the last hope of the people too got badly shattered by the leaders' deviation from their early commitments to their ideology and ideals. In the extreme irritation and frustration, I thought that I should remain absent from those inconsistencies of the Nepalese political scenario for some time. I have been utilizing this time on a good amount of writing which I am now doing in Canada. In one year in Canada I wrote three books **Rebels of the Mountains** (2011), **Beyond the Life Lines** (2011), and **Between Roars and Rigors** and got them published from America. An intellectual has many more ways to survive in the world. In an under developed country if the politicians are not honest, mere intellectuals can do very little for the people.

The reminiscences of Nepalese history of the conflicts that I have jutted down here are not wholly chronological and research-based like the work of a sincere historian. They have been constantly reeling up in my mind from which I have dared to selectively write down the most striking ones only. I could have written them more systematically and even more minutely and interestingly, and I will definitely do it sometime later.

Over this time I have come to know from the history of Nepal that the divinization of a leader is very harmful for himself, for the people, for the country and for a revolutionary party too. Another thing I have realized is that Nepal does not need an over-smart leader as its executive head, but a straightforward, sincere and devoted personality. Let's hope that every situation is paving way for the rise of a genuine leadership who loves the country and truly respects the aspiration of the people.

Chapter Twenty
The Times I Wept

I have wept in my life probably a countless times. Weeping is said to be the first language of a human being. Apart from the times I have wept with my parents, I have wept with my equals and juniors too quite a number of times affected by the sudden strikes of shocks and also by the gusts of pleasures.

The news about the murder of poet Krishna Sen 'Ichchhuk' was really intolerable for me. He was a very good man; gentle, soft spoken, committed, friendly and sensible. On hearing about his murder I wept a lot all day and night long. I could not imagine that such a good man too could be killed by the police and army just because of his ideological stand. The point from which he thought about justice, welfare, progress, equality, fraternity and solidarity could be a crime to the regressive elements and to the fascists. I could not bear it, and emitted out my feeling of shocks through a river of tears. Like me, many other people who knew him must have wept on his remembrance. Any commemoration, obituary and elegy would be insufficient to dedicate to such a good person. In my shock and anger I wrote about his life and literary creations and published for the knowledge and attention of the people of the world. Similarly, I have cried over the deaths and injuries of many good hearts and minds.

I cannot remember all those moments when I have wept. I say that I am not a man that weeps frequently on all small happenings. In that sense I say that I am quite stern and enduring from my inside. I generally don't weep even when others are weeping. I will be the man to console, sympathize and encourage people for endurance and advancement at troubles and sorrows. But when I myself wept which means that it must have been a very extraordinary situation. I did not weep even with the news of my father's death.

One afternoon in a cold day in Kathmandu, I had been to a friend's office. Only when I had entered the office compartment, my cell phone rang. My brother from home about five hundred kilometres away from Kathmandu had called me. "Brother! Our father suddenly fell sick. We lifted him up and brought to the balcony of the house. He has fainted. We are trying to bring him to consciousness. Kedar dai and Makunda dai are rubbing his feet."

I told him "Call an ambulance quickly and inform another brother in Biratnagar. Take the father to the nearest health centre and then to the hospital. Report it to me at every ten minutes."

After ten minutes I received his call again. "Yes, he gained consciousness. Govinda is coming with an ambulance. We are getting him to wear the dress to rush him to the hospital."

After another ten minutes I called the brother. He said, "We are waiting for the ambulance to come. He has put on the dress. Mother too is preparing to go. She is getting the bags ready to stay in the hospital at night."

After twenty minutes I received a call from the brother. "The ambulance is in front of the house but the father does not want to go."

I exclaimed, "Why? What happened? He must go? Convince him. Get him ready. He requires a quick treatment. The doctors have to check him. Convince him."

The bother replied, "No, he does not want to go. He says it is useless."

I got shocked. I said, "Can you give him the phone? I talk to him myself."

The brother reported, "He does not want to talk. He says that you should come back home soon."

The brother shouted and screamed. "Oh! See! What happened to the father! O, my god! He is dead!" Then I heard on the phone that everybody started crying loudly. Another brother told me that the father was dead, so that we all should come home from Kathmandu as soon as possible.

I told my friend Mr. Bishnu Pukar, in whose office I had just been half an hour ago, about my bad luck. He sympathised me in complete sadness. No sooner had I had the chance to say hello to him than I started getting busy on the phone calls. I said bye to him and got out in haste.

I went home straight and told my wife about the incident. Then I gave call to my brothers to come to my home quickly telling them clearly about the death of the father. My second, third and fourth brothers were in Kathmandu living with their families. They gathered at my place. By that time it was about six in the evening. Then we wanted to have money. The banks were closed. None of us had the ATM cards then. Upon a call my second brother's friends Purna and Umesh brought him some twenty thousand rupees.

There was no bus to the eastern Nepal at that time. We had to wait for the following day only. I asked Manoj brother to reserve at least four plane tickets for us. Unfortunately, all plane tickets were reserved by others for several days to come, and because of the thick fogs in the sky, the planes had not flown to the eastern plain lands for some days. The bus route too had been obstructed when the flood in Koshi River had broken the eastern side dam, and several villages of Nepal and India were badly flooded away. The local fisher men had made a temporary bamboo bridge over the branch of the river. The bus would only reach some kilometres before the flooded area.

Manoj brother collected four tickets for different flights. From early in the morning next day, we four brothers, leaving our families behind, rustled at the air port terminal, but none of the planes had a single flight till the late afternoon. We waited, waited and waited hopelessly looking at the sky to see if the fog was being clear. Kathmandu's sky was a bit clear, but the tower informed that the Biratnagar airport was still covered with thick fog.

We received phone calls from the cousins every half an hour. At about 2 p.m., we were informed that it was unwise to keep the dead body in that way. We gave our consent for the funeral procession to the cremation of the dead body. People prepared for the procession. The conch was loudly blown on the phone for us to hear that funeral procession started. My heart inflated with emotion of shock thinking that I could not meet my father at the last moments of his life, nor could I have the sight of his face in the end, nor could I attend the funeral procession. On hearing the sound of conch-blow, I could not resist myself. Then, in front of everyone at the airport terminal, I suddenly burst out in tears. My brothers too shed tears beside me.

Then we caught a night bus in haste, and with much difficulty we reached the point of the Koshi barrage. We caught a private vehicle as far as to the bamboo bridge where we had to pay in order to walk across. Then, from a little bit farther, we took a taxi for about sixty kilometres away to our home village.

We had to follow the traditional process right from the river where the father's dead body was burnt. Our relatives had been already there. We had to shave the hair clean to total baldness, and we did. A brother of mine who had been lost for ten years had just arrived at the river side a few minutes before we reached there. Then, by our cousins and relatives we were escorted home.

To see us at home everybody wept, cried, moaned, and lamented over the death of the father. I consoled everybody that the shock has to be borne thinking that death is an inevitable process, and everybody has to die sooner or later. I asked the people around how everything happened so soon to the father.

People there told us that father was playing cards almost all day long that day at the resting shed. Some hours ago the long lost brother of mine had given him a call that he would be coming home soon. His long disappearance had remained a deep shock in the father's mind almost like a trauma. While playing cards also, he was telling the people there that his long lost son would be coming home soon. He was feeling ecstatically excited by the idea of his coming back home. After the game of cards he invited everybody that they should come to play the games next day also. When he was coming home just fifty meters away from the shed; he fell down on the way. He had the heart attack. He was rushed home, but when he got up, he had the second stroke and he died. Everybody deduced that he felt over excited by the idea of his long lost son's arrival, and he got the attack.

On hearing every story how my father died so suddenly, I burst out in tears again. I deeply felt the absence of my father. My father had all the great qualities of a superman. Deeply remembering the father, I wept as much as I could.

Would you like to see your manuscript become a book?

If you are interested in becoming a PublishAmerica author, please submit your manuscript for possible publication to us at:

acquisitions@publishamerica.com

You may also mail in your manuscript to:

**PublishAmerica
PO Box 151
Frederick, MD 21705**

www.publishamerica.com

CPSIA information can be obtained at www.ICGtesting.com
Printed in the USA
LVOW12s1922251013

358638LV00001B/164/P